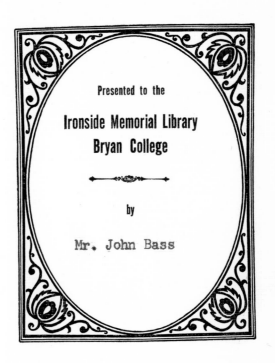

The Empty Pulpit

Gerald Whiteman Gillaspie

moody press
chicago

ISBN: 0-8024-2342-6

Printed in the United States of America

Contents

5

Foreword

From time to time those church bodies with a congregational form of government are faced with the responsibility of calling a pastor. This is one of the most significant decisions which will confront a congregation. Because it involves finding a leader whose influence will determine in large measure the future of that particular church, it places a serious obligation on both the congregation and the search committee.

The author of *The Empty Pulpit* has in a previous book, *The Restless Pastor*, shown a perceptiveness and sensitivity in giving valuable counsel to the undershepherd. Now in addressing himself to the procurement of a pastor, his practical insights and instructions have provided a valuable service for the congregational type of church.

From his research of biblical concepts, historical patterns, and current trends has emerged some basic principles which must be observed. Again, he has outlined orderly procedures which if followed will obviate uncertainty and tension which may easily arise under these circumstances.

The appendices which include a self-study form, together with other sample letters, will give valuable guidance to those who are called to serve in this capacity.

Mr. Gillaspie's book belongs in every church library and merits advance consideration before the actual need arises. Careful study will enable church leaders who may have this responsibility only once in their Christian experience to move with certainty and objectivity in this all-important matter of calling a pastor.

WARREN R. MAGNUSON

Preface

This book includes a critical look at the candidating procedures for pastoral procurement and placement practiced by many Protestant, self-governing evangelical churches of the United States and Canada. Its purpose is to provide meaningful guidelines to assist churches and pastors in improving existing policies for a more intelligent and efficient use, so that pastors chosen will be the ones best suited to particular churches. Although the undergirding statistical study was with two denominations—The Evangelical Free Church of America and the Baptist General Conference—the book is written to assist all self-governing churches.

The author wishes to acknowledge his indebtedness to Lloyd M. Perry, Division Chairman, Department of Practical Theology, Trinity Evangelical Divinity School, for his encouragement and ready assistance. He wishes also to express his indebtedness to others who assisted in preparing and mailing 1,572 questionnaire forms. A special note of appreciation is given to his wife, who helped in many ways, and did all the tabulation of the 625 questionnaires returned.

9

Introduction

The present candidating procedures practiced by many churches in securing pastors have changed very little over the past seventy-five years. There is a need to evaluate this procedure in light of the complexity of today's pastoral responsibilities and the broadened ministry of the church. The question is, Has the candidating procedure kept pace with the changing roles of pastor and church? The place and ministry of the pastor is not the same today as even twenty-five years ago. It is possible that the traditional pattern used to secure a pastor for a local church is not adequate to choose a pastor today. Most contemporary pastors often have to oversee the finances of the church, help direct the Christian education programs, guide expansion programs, and be responsible for hiring and firing staff personnel. This is quite different from the itinerant minister whose major responsibility was to preach. Because of this, he was often called "the preacher," and the principal consideration in calling a pastor was his preaching ability. Yet today the same "trial sermon" is often the sole criteria for a church in calling a pastor. The traditional candidating procedure has simply not kept pace with the change in pastoral responsibilities.

The key question that must be faced is, How can the traditional candidating procedure practiced by most self-governing churches become more efficient in the light of current pastoral responsibilities, and hence a keener instrument by which the Holy Spirit can guide the right pastor to the church best suited to his abilities and gifts? This is especially pertinent when we recognize there is no definite policy practiced even within specific denominations. Confusion is evident with no careful procedure determined. As long ago as 1935, William R. McNutt called for reform, but few paid much attention to his plea.* Of course the problem is primarily related to the self-governing churches, not to those whose pastors are placed by hierarchical control. There is, however, an increasing number of churches with central control who are giving more and more authority to the local congregations. Thus the need for guidelines in the candidating procedure becomes broader.

The need for a definitive work in this area is evident because so many churches and pastors have failed to arrive at productive relationships. Many have floundered by entering a relationship on a "hope for the best" basis. Many churches have followed the candidating procedure without adequate understanding of why or how it can work effectively. The role of the pulpit committee has not been well understood, nor its work properly outlined.

Some denominations have booklets or pamphlets on the subject, but others admit that they have very little assistance to offer. Of twelve denominations surveyed who use the congregational system of government, six have no printed helps, and three admit that they do very little to guide their churches and/or pastors in this crucial decision. One denomination leader said, "We have grown up with the system of candidating pastors and I am sure we take many things for granted. We have no printed instructions on the subject." Because of this lack of recent writing on the subject, most of

---

*"A pastorless church in quest of a man to shepherd the flock has no definite policy to guide it. Every method conceivable is in operation in the denomination (Baptist). The greatest confusion and utter lack of studied procedure reign at this crucial point. The rapid increase of ministerial supply makes it incumbent that the churches now work out some efficient and dignified method of finding the desired men and of extending the call. Lack of a stable polity creates a condition unfair to the ministry and hazardous for the churches" (William R. McNutt, *Polity and Practices in Baptist Churches* [Philadelphia: Judson, 1935], p. 82).

the authorities quoted in this book lived as long as a hundred years ago. The reader, however, will be encouraged to note that church leaders of today are in general agreement with their statements.

It is evident that denominations should launch instructional programs in the candidating procedure for both churches and pastors. Such instruction could be given at a workshop during a denominational annual meeting or be adopted as a project of lay fellowships or ministerial associations.

This book is written with the hope that it will assist pastors, churches, and denominations in making pastoral candidating the sacred and careful procedure that God intended it to be.

1

Historical Basis and Current Trends of Pastoral Placement and Procurement

THE CHURCH AND ITS PASTOR—A SACRED RELATIONSHIP

The pastor of a visible, local church relates to the church as the undershepherd of the Great Shepherd, Christ Himself. Christ promised to provide undershepherds for His Church (Eph 4:11-12) to assist in this process of perfecting the Church. Therefore the pastor's relationship to the church is vital and sacred—a relationship that should only be entered into after careful consideration and prayer. It is not a relationship to be gained by crude or chance procedures.

BIBLICAL PRINCIPLES AND THE CANDIDATING PROCEDURE

The question before us is, "How is the pastor-people relationship inaugurated?" Does the Bible give any guidelines for the church to follow in procuring a pastor? One question in the survey used in gathering data for this book was, "Does the concept of candidating have any biblical foundation?" Hundreds of pastors and church leaders appeared to be somewhat frantic in attempting to give biblical undergirding to the candidating procedure. Many New Testament verses were listed. Even a few Old Testament passages were provided. In examining the Scripture, it is quite apparent that appointment was the basic practice in the early church pastoral placement (Ac 14:23; 1 Co 4:17; Phil 2:19, 25, 28; 1 Th 3:2;

15

1 Ti 1:3; 2 Ti 4:12; Titus 1:5). A few men candidly stated
that much of church government is based on the necessity of
the particular case, not specific verses of Scripture. The New
Testament indicates quite clearly that pastors at first came
from within the local church. The fact that the New Testament church situation usually involved the founding of
churches precluded the possibility of candidating. We must
conclude that the Bible does not specifically support the candidating procedure, but neither does it forbid or deny it.
Church government procedures have had to be developed in
many areas in the absence of direct biblical guidance. Many,
nevertheless, have been built on biblical principles. The candidating procedure is no exception. The autonomy of the
local congregation is a New Testament principle that not only
girds the candidating procedure but is honored by it.

ADMINISTRATIVE PHILOSOPHY AND PRINCIPLES OF
THE EARLY CHURCH

The Bible also does not give us any indication of an authori-
tative council to delegate available pastors to empty pulpits.
Such a council would not be compatible with the autonomy
of the local church. Certain principles followed by the apostolic churches should, however, indicate an acceptable procedure which was blessed of God in the rapid growth of the
Church, and thus should be followed today simply because
we know it has been pragmatically approved by God.

To find such principles, a study of the early New Testament
Church is necessary. In 1 Corinthians 14, written twenty-five
years after our Lord's crucifixion, we have a picture, from the
apostle Paul himself, of a Christian service in one of his
churches. It is the earliest and most authentic testimony we
have on the subject. Paul states that every Christian has
received the Holy Spirit and some gift of the Spirit. Whatever gift a man possesses, it was given primarily for the general good of the church (1 Co 12:4-7; Eph 4:11-16). Thus,

the form of the church service depended upon the nature of the gifts of those present. Usually there would be prayer, praise, and teaching or preaching along with the reading of the Word (i.e., Old Testament). Paul certainly gives his approval to the congregation directing its own service and ministry. Was this a new idea or was there some rootage to it? There is no doubt that Christian services were originally modeled on the lines of the Jewish synagogue service and have never fully departed from it.[1] We must not forget that the members of the First Church at Jerusalem were Jews in their religious worship and, for many years, loyal to the customs of their fathers (Ac 21:20).

In the Jewish synagogue, the service consisted of opening sentences, prayers spoken by one of the congregation, lessons from Scripture read by different members of the congregation, and the exposition of a passage of Scripture by the reader or someone else. This is the key to the Christian services as described in 1 Corinthians 14, and in all the apostolic churches practically to the end of the first century.

Each Christian church was a true brotherhood where the Spirit alone reigned supreme. Any idea of even the apostles lording it over the "brethren" was excluded (2 Co 1:24; 1 Pe 5:1-3). "But be not ye called Rabbi: for one is your Master, even Christ; and all ye are brethren" (Mt 23:8). It was upon this principle that each church was self-governing. Every author investigated directly or indirectly in this study admits to this original self-governing principle for local congregations.

The Bible clearly indicates that the early Christians understood this scriptural principle of local church independence. Matthew 18:15-17 contains instructions given by the Lord for the settlement of controversies between members of a local church. First the differences are to be resolved between the individuals if possible. If no reconciliation is accomplished, a second attempt is to be made with one or two witnesses. Third, if he will not hear them, "tell it unto the church." And if he will not hear the local church, there is no higher court but God. By the action of the church, he is to be refused fellowship until he demonstrates the reality of his faith by confession of his sin. Then he is to be restored, as taught in Galatians 6:1. Thus in the matter of discipline there is no earthly authority higher than the local congregation. This being the case, the local church certainly has the right to call its own pastor.

Acts 15 gives the account of the settlement of a crucial doctrinal matter. Again the local church is the final court of appeal. No man or institution can come between the believer and his God. Every believer is a king, prophet, and priest to God (1 Pe 2:5, 9; Rev 1:6; 5:10). Of course, it is impossible for any society or church to do without officers. If the prayers, praise, teaching, and acts of congregational worship are to be done decently and in order, the congregation must appoint one (or more) of its number to be the delegated spokesman by whom these acts may be led or performed. Churches can function without a pastor; however they function better with one.

In seeking a pastor, the local church may, of course, request assistance. District or national church leaders are available for recommendations and information, but the authority always lies in the hands of the people. The church may search for a pastor completely independent of any outside help, but there is a trend among the congregationally governed churches to seek denominational assistance. Some of the more progressive churches feel that assistance from district or national leaders within the denomination is almost essential. Denominational leaders of congregationally governed churches encourage this because they sincerely feel that they possess certain information and knowledge vital to churches seeking pastors.*

---

*Denominational leaders of the Evangelical Free Church of America and the Baptist General Conference, whose churches govern themselves independently, indicate that more and more churches are seeking denominational help, and that the denominations welcome this.

Summary

The early churches based on the Jewish synagogue administration were self-governing. Innately related to this was the selection of their own pastors. The congregational form of government has historical and biblical roots and gives the basis for procurement of a pastor by the candidating procedure.

2

The Candidating Policy

HISTORICAL RELATIONSHIPS

We have already seen that the procedure of procuring a pastor for a church by the candidating method is directly related to the type of church government which allows local autonomy. Because of this relationship, the procedure has biblical roots deep in Church history.[1] Church annals are filled with accounts of the church exercising its authority to ordain. Certainly, therefore, it has the authority to call and dismiss its pastors.*

PERMANENCE OF THE PROCEDURE AND ITS ADVANTAGES

The roots of the candidating policy are so deep and so closely entwined with the democratic government of such churches that there is little reason to believe that it will ever be discarded for another procedure. Interviews with pastors and denominational leaders indicate that the procedure is here to stay, but that we can expect some reevaluation and modification of it in order to take it from the area of "chance" to a meaningful and efficient procedure used by God to place the right man in the right church. The choice of a pastor by a church is a priority concern. Hiscox says that the selection and election of a pastor is one of the most, if not the most,

---

*"As the local church is competent to ordain, so it is also competent to call and dismiss its own minister" (William R. McNutt, *Polity and Practice in Baptist Churches,* p. 82).

important acts pertaining to the independence of the church. "The interest of the body, and the welfare of religion depend so largely on it, that it should be entered upon with the utmost care, deliberation, and prayer for divine direction."[2] It is the only procedure that allows the whole church to express a consensus by the Holy Spirit in the selection of its pastor.

No other procedure of pastoral procurement throws the church together and in dependence upon God as does the candidating procedure. Certainly the congregation will pray that divine guidance be given to the appointing bishop in churches where this is the policy. But there cannot be the same sense of urgency and dire need of divine wisdom as when the sole responsibility lies with the church. The candidating method gets the church personally involved; it gives the congregation a voice. This can bring a sense of responsibility to the people of the church; a desire to cooperate with and support the man they choose. A favorable vote is generally a commitment to cooperate. This method of selecting a pastor allows the church to select a pastor according to its need. No one should know the needs of a church better than the church itself; but many churches have never determined a philosophy of existence and thus may need objective outside help in defining its biblical purpose and objectives.

There are also certain benefits to the candidate himself. One pastor stated, "Having served one pastorate under a conference assignment procedure, I find that candidating is more democratic and mutually satisfying to both pastor and people alike." Another said, "I was a Methodist pastor for seven years and feel it [candidating] is superior, for we feel now that the people want us and are not having us forced upon them. You are *their* pastor after you are called."

The necessity of candidating may awaken a minister out of his lethargy and require him to change his preaching style and message content to meet the needs of different people. He faces a new challenge that can bring him closer to God and develop hidden abilities. He enters the arena with others, and the verdict is given him on the basis of personal merit. The pastor who desires to do more for God will thank Him when necessity forces him to reevaluate his ministry, strengthen the weak places, and utilize to a greater degree his personal strengths. Occasional candidating can have this effect.

Further benefit to the candidate comes when he appreciates that such a call from a local church is also a call of God, for it is God who rules the affairs of His church, and especially in so important a matter as the selection of its spiritual guide. The procedure urges the church and the candidate to reach out in faith toward God in a way no other procedure does.

DANGERS AND DISADVANTAGES

As in every case, good things can be perverted. The democratic method has some built-in dangers. With the advantage of independence must come a sense of grave responsibility that the privileges are not misused.

SEPARATENESS WEAKENS UNITY

Independence from a centralized ecclesiastical authority can produce a feeling of separateness that weakens the tie which ought to bind the individual church to others of its own communion. This is especially so when a local church finds it necessary to go outside its own denomination to obtain a pastor. The Home Missions Secretary of one denomination stated that every effort should be made by the local church to choose men from within its own ranks. Experience has proven that doing otherwise often results in many problems to the church.

THE TRANSIENT PREACHER

There is the risk that the church will make its choice without adequate information. There is also danger of exposing the church to exploitation by unworthy candidates. Another denominational leader emphasized the danger involved with transient preachers. They have a couple of very fine sermons and can sway a congregation, but they are "gypsy preachers" because they have no leadership and administrative ability. These are usually the preachers who personally apply and flippantly state that "God is leading me to your church." The pastorless church should beware of such men.

PREACHING ABILITY MADE THE ONLY CRITERIA FOR CHOICE

There is always the danger that the pulpit committee and/ or church will make its decision only on the basis of impressions gained from hearing a sermon or two. Most Protestant churches lay too much stress upon the candidate's preaching ability† and give inadequate consideration to other vitally important areas such as his training, experience, quality of his pastoral and administrative work, and respect in the community. The most stirring pulpiteer does not necessarily make the most satisfactory pastor. Solid and durable qualities of character and commitment are certainly more important than the single ability to "display all one's goods in the shop window."³ All denominational leaders interviewed reiterated this danger of making a decision only on the basis of hearing a sermon or two. The church should understand and appreciate that the preaching of a man grows on them. The Baptist General Conference advocates that a candidate spend at least a long weekend with the church considering him. Ideally the minister should spend a week or two, if feasible, getting to know the church and its people.‡ Not only is there the

†Although Worth does temper the following statement by other comments in his book, he does emphatically say, "A candidate is in competition with preachers or heralds. If he fails here, he fails at the crucial place. And if he cannot come recommended as a preacher of some ability, the church will hardly seriously consider him. He must have some exceptional qualification to offset his lack in the really important place. . . . We forgive and overlook a hundred defects if a man has a message" (Horace Worth, *The Art of Candidating* [Boston: Printed for private circulation, 1907], pp. 35-36).

‡Where it is possible a short probationary period of a month or more will lessen the possibility of a mistake being made either by the church or the ministry . . . but such a probationary ministry is only possible to the minister without a charge or to a student about to enter the work of the ministry" (T. Harwood Pattison, *For the Work of the Ministry* [Philadelphia: Amer. Bapt. Pubn. Soc., 1907], pp. 66-67).

danger of slecting a man on the basis of his superficial attrac-
tiveness, but also sometimes the sheer weariness of a congregation exhausted by reviewing an endless line of major
and minor prophets brings them to the place of grasping at
the next man.[4]

There is no doubt that some candidating ministers are
placed in demanding situations. But this is usually due to a
lack of careful planning and procedure on the part of the
pastor and the church or pulpit committee. Nothing calls
forth the true character of Christian men and women more
than does this situation. It provides opportunity for brothers
in Christ to act in open integrity.

The problems encountered are not due to the procedure itself, but to its misuse. Both ministers and churches need to
be educated as to the expanded intricacies of the candidating
procedure—that the procedure involves more than hearing a
man speak once or twice and shaking his hand. This expanded
candidating procedure, discussed in subsequent chapters,
offers benefit to both the minister and the congregation by
providing opportunity for mutual, in-depth acquaintance.
But the one- or two-sermon approach is fraught with problems. It is impossible to judge on such meager evidence how
well a man will wear, what reserves he has, what tact, insight,
scholarship, moral courage, what self-effacing loyalty and
devotion. Yet these qualities are certainly as essential in a
good minister as a good voice, an attractive pulpit presence,
and one or two good sermons. Obviously something needs to
be done about the practices still followed by many churches
today.

OPTIONS AND MODIFICATIONS

The survey of 268 churches and 334 pastors indicates that
no change in the basic candidating policy is desired or expected. It also indicates that many churches still depend,
almost solely, on just hearing a man preach. Following are
some quotes from the survey: "We invite a pastor to speak,

and the congregational meeting is held to vote." "The pulpit committee goes out, and they hear prospective candidates. Then they call a prospect for a tryout. Then the members vote." "Candidate comes and has a service. Church body votes to call or not to call." "He has a service with us, and we have a business meeting to vote on whether to call him as our pastor." "We invite those candidating to preach in our church, and the congregation then makes their choice on one." One pastor sent a tape and a large picture of himself to a church about 1,000 miles away. These were used for a morning service. Another church called a pastor from England on the strength of a taped sermon. It turned out to be the only good sermon he had. A pastor said, "I have candidated at churches where all I did was speak. I was given no opportunity to talk to the board, and neither did the board desire to talk to me. In all but one case I got the call."

All this emphasizes how important it is for the procedure to be upgraded and improved to fit the context of the modern pastoral position. We must provide safeguards against the possible dangers and abuses, and construct guidelines for the administration of the method to maximum efficiency under God. Before proceeding to such guidelines, a brief examination should be made of some suggested options or modifications to the candidating procedure. Many have made a plea for a change because of its misuse. But very few have made meaningful suggestions for another procedure that fits the historical New Testament policy of autonomous church government.

USE OF A COMPUTER

The most current option is one designed to use data processing. *Moody Monthly* magazine provided the following news release: "A personnel management system will replace the old 'preaching for a call method of assigning clergymen in the United Church of Canada.' The new approach for handling ministers may include a proposed information recall and referral system, which could be central, national and computerized."[5] The Lutheran Church/Missouri Synod is advocating the use of a computer for pastoral placement.[6]

THE REPRESENTATIVE COMMITTEE

Washington Gladden is somewhat hesitant about the candidating procedure and feels that if a candidate is a man well-known in all the churches, such an exhibition of himself seems quite superfluous. Gladden doubts the expediency of it even if the candidate is not well-known.[7] Thus he suggests, "On the whole, it is not only less embarrassing for the minister, but wiser for the church, if the whole matter be entrusted to a large and judicious committee, upon whose report, without further investigation, the church consents to act."[8]

CHOICE ON THE MINISTER'S RECORD ALONE

One pastor who has completed fifty years in the Evangelical Free Church of America stated that of the six churches he has served, five called him on the basis of his record alone, without candidating. Others have had similar experiences. Distance and cost sometimes preclude the possibility of actual on-location candidating. Careful investigation coupled with much prayer has been sufficient to enable some churches to make right decisions, but there are dangers in this approach. The candidate suffers from this procedure because he does not have the opportunity to see the church for himself and to feel the atmosphere of its people. There is nothing that provides the church and the minister more thorough initial acquaintance than the actual candidating visit based upon serious investigation beforehand. The personal candidating encounter of pastor and church has no meaningful substitute.

SCOUTING BY THE SUB-COMMITTEE

One modification of the candidating method used quite extensively is for the pulpit committee to appoint a smaller executive committee to do the scouting and to bring back reports. This eliminates the necessity of the whole committee to invade a church and turn the morning worship into an unexpected candidating encounter. A large pulpit committee can be identified too easily, so the minister is then not really heard under normal conditions. If the church is not too distant, one or two committee members may be able to visit the church and hear the minister on different Sundays. This enables the committee to compare notes of a broader exposure to the minister, and it does not upset the church with an identified pulpit committee present. If the church of the prospective pastor is a considerable distance away, one representative of the committee may be appointed to travel (at the church's expense) to hear him. Although not as meaningful, McNutt has suggested that friends of committeemen living near the church may be asked to visit the church and report their findings.[9]

DENOMINATIONAL HELP

Supplementing the candidating process with denominational assistance has already been mentioned and is an augmentation that Dobbins advocates. He says, "Another forward step would be constructive denominational concern for the problem."[10] As a Baptist he recognizes the danger and difficulty this may entail for autonomous churches. But he also states that no satisfactory plan has yet been devised for churches to place the procurement of pastors in hands other than their own, without surrendering one of their most precious privileges.

THE MINISTERIAL BUREAU

An office of pastoral supply is also suggested by Dobbins as a clearinghouse through which information concerning pastorless churches could be secured by churchless pastors (or by pastors seeking a change) and vice versa.[11] This is no new idea. It was advocated years ago, but in a little more extensive way. Gladden, in the year 1887, had two lengthy paragraphs given to the idea of a ministerial bureau or committee of ministerial exchange to serve as a medium of communication between churches desiring ministers and ministers wanting churches.[12] This appears to be a feasible plan and yet, as Gladden says, when the method is tried, it does not produce the desired result. A great northern Presbyterian church experimented with it but with discouraging results.[13]

As far back as 1907, Worth commented quite extensively on this idea and spoke as if most denominations of his time had such a clearinghouse.[14] The problems of such a bureau would probably be legion, and pressures from pastors and churches could present more problems than solutions. The answer may lie in a balance or mingling of ideas. Even Worth says that the bureau of pastoral supply is not to be recommended as a sole reliance and that its value lies in supplementing the work done by others.[15] The bureau should act more as a consulting committee than one with authority. Many denominations have leaders or committees that take on this responsibility without actually designating the committee by name. *Christian Life* magazine of November 1961 has a brief news article concerning a current approach to this idea.[16] "The Church Service Agency is making itself available as a means of communication between churches seeking ministers and ministers who may be willing to consider the possibility of pastoral changes." This agency could be especially helpful to independent churches and to ministers who usually serve in nondenominational churches. *Christian Life* magazine provided the latest address of the Church Service Agency, but when a letter was sent to that address it was returned with the notation from the post office, "Box closed, no order." Apparently another attempt at a pastoral placement bureau failed.

Need for Modification

This study of possible options or modifications simply underscores that the candidating procedure is the only policy really acceptable to the autonomous church. Admittedly there are misuses, dangers, and problems. Therefore, it is imperative to determine procedural guidelines to ensure optimum usage of this accepted policy.

Summary

The candidating policy is rooted in the history of the Church. There is no indication that it will be replaced by another method in self-governing churches. There is, however, a call to improve the method for a more intelligent, efficient use. Dangers must be recognized and averted as the advantages are fully utilized.

3

Guidelines for the Church

THE PASTOR-CHURCH RELATIONSHIP IS MORE THAN AN EMPLOYEE-EMPLOYER RELATIONSHIP

Before the pulpit committee can function effectively, the church must accept the biblical role of the pastor, and thus establish a right attitude toward the pastoral relationship.

The church must dismiss from its mind the idea that it is *hiring a pastor!* Although some well-meaning men will probably always speak of hiring a minister, the idea is not in keeping with the biblical role of a pastor. The church which sets about to "hire" a minister has never determined a philosophy of the local church, nor made a careful examination of the pastor's role as described in the Word of God. To hire a pastor carries with it the understanding that the pastor is employed by the people to do the work assigned to the church.

This allows the church to become observers rather than participants. Ephesians 4:12 succinctly states that the pastor is to prepare God's people for the work of the ministry. When the church realizes this and the sacredness of such a position, it will carefully plan to "call" a pastor, but not to "hire" a minister. Legally, of course, his written call to a local church and his written acceptance of the call constitute a contract. But the services he is to render are of such a character that the word "hire" is not appropriate. "Surely, one cannot associate the word 'hiring' with the making of a solemn covenant

30

between a man that is to shepherd souls and the souls that he is to shepherd."[1] The use of the word *hire* reflects a wrong attitude on the part of the church:

> The minister is not an "hireling of the sheep" but a shepherd of the flock; not an "hired man" on wages whose employment may be terminated on brief notice, but a professional man in a sacred calling of standing and dignity. A state does not "hire" a governor, nor a city a mayor, nor a university a professor. Neither should a church debase the ministry by attempting to "hire" a pastor.[2]

COURTESY DUE THE SISTER CHURCH

Another area that a pastorless church often overlooks because of its intense concern for itself is its obligation and courtesy to other churches whose pastors it is considering. The church without a pastor must appreciate something of the difficult situation in which it may be placing another church and its pastor when it starts to consult with that pastor about the possibility of candidating. Love and concern for the sister churches must prevail. Often this is not even considered, and some ill feelings result. Openness and honesty motivated by love should be the policy. The church in need of a pastor must recognize that when a call is extended to a pastor of another church, that pastor then has two calls to consider. His present church extended him a call and it is still just as valid as the new call.

Harmon solves this problem quite easily by advising that no church make overtures to a pastor who has not resigned, and if they do, such overtures should not be considered by the employed pastor. He bases this advice on the Congregational, Presbyterian, and Unitarian Code for Pastors.* How-

---

* "'It is unethical for a minister to make overtures to or consider overtures from a Church whose pastor has not yet resigned.' (Congregational Code, III, 3; Presbyterian Code almost identical.) 'He should discourage all overtures from a Church whose minister has not yet resigned.' (Unitarian Code, IV, 3)" (Nolan B. Harmon, *Understanding the Methodist Church* [Nashville: Meth. Pub., 1955], p. 122).

ever ethical this may seem, in practice it is untenable. Certainly it is best not to disturb with overtures of interest a pastor who is happily and productively at work. Yet this cannot be adopted as a maxim. Paul may have been contentedly working at Troas, but the vision of the man from Macedonia who said, "Come over into Macedonia and help us," (Ac 16:9) constrained him to depart. In such cases the voice of the people may be the voice of God. Gladden states well that "no church possesses any exclusive right to any minister."[3] In such a difficult situation a great deal depends on how the subject is broached, and what sort of spirit is maintained. The interests of God's will for His whole church must be paramount:

> Every church must proceed in this business with a deep and prayerful sense of its responsibility, not for its own welfare alone, but for the interests of its sister church and of the Kingdom of Heaven. To build itself up by pulling down other churches is not the principle on which it is founded. It is surely possible for a Christian church to understand and observe, in its relations with its sister churches, the law of Christ the Lord.[4]

A church which considers a minister already settled elsewhere is under moral obligation to deal courteously and fairly with its sister church. Certain guidelines may be listed: 1. A church should not make overtures to a minister who has recently settled in a new church, unless it is known that the new relationship has proven unsatisfactory. Even then, it may be in order to give that church a fair chance to work out solutions and solve the problems. 2. A large and rich church should not flaunt its material strength and offer a much larger salary than the minister is receiving on condition that he come immediately. Every church must appreciate that a minister has certain obligations to his present church, and that his agreement (contract) obligates him to give a certain amount of notice to the church. It cannot be expected that a pastor drop his ministry in the middle of a seasonal effort or special thrust. He must be given opportunity to bring his pastorate to a dignified conclusion. Also, a certain amount of time is needed by the other church to adjust itself and to make plans to call another pastor. 3. Common courtesy would also dictate that no church should call a man from another pulpit without giving the church where he is already serving full opportunity to counsel with their pastor and honestly talk over the option of remaining. "It is not well that a Christian church should follow the methods of the children of Dan in their seduction of the priest of the house of Micah."[5] The Lutheran Church/Missouri Synod suggests that the pastorless church write the church whose pastor it has called in the following manner. "Having called upon our Lord for guidance, we have elected your pastor to assume the pastoral office in our midst. We ask that you consider this most important decision with him, that you pray with and for him, and that, if you find it to be the Lord's will that he accept our call, you grant him a release."[6]

Pastoral Idealisms

Churches should also appreciate that a minister will never be able to please everyone. The ministry of a pastor includes administration, preaching, teaching, evangelizing, and counseling. No administrator, prophet, teacher, evangelist, or counselor has ever, in religious history, done his work fearlessly in the sight of God and pleased everybody. The minister does have a special calling, but he is human and subject to the same temptations and problems as other men. We must not forget that pastors are human. Paul so reminds the people of Lystra (Ac 14:15), and James so speaks of Elijah (Ja 5:17).

Engage in a Self-Study

The church, before it starts to look for a pastor, should adopt a brief self-study by an appointed committee, or delegate this responsibility to the pulpit committee (see pp. 62-

67). The purpose of such a study is to identify the needs of
the church. How else can a church intelligently seek a pastor
to meet its needs?† "Far too often a pastorless church will
seek another pastor from a larger field of service, and offer
great inducements prior to his acceptance of the call. Churches have sought successful men, or younger men of charm and
great personality—it is such a human failing—without considering the needs of the parish. Is the call to a Christian church
parish to be considered on the elements of salary, prestige or
material 'offers'? Or is the first need that should be considered that of the spiritual needs of the parish?"[7] The primary
objective should always be to find a man whose particular
gifts and abilities may have the amplest opportunity for expression because they parallel the needs of the church. A man
thoroughly trained and of good qualifications and experience
may fail in one church where he does not fit, yet be thoroughly successful in another. The church should not reject a man
just because he has had a failure. He may not have been
suited to that church. Some men serve better in country
churches than in city or suburban churches, and vice versa.
This point needs emphasis because one failure in a pastorate
often causes a church seeking a pastor to automatically eliminate that man from its list of potential candidates. Such a
man may not have adapted to that church, or was ill-equipped
to solve its problems. He no doubt is a good, sound man and
may do well in a church where he fits. Here the help of district or national denominational leaders can be of valuable
assistance. They know why the man failed and can advise a
church about him.

SEEK DENOMINATIONAL HELP

This leads us to another guideline for churches—seek denominational help. The calling of a pastor marks a most seri-

---

†"The expressed needs of the churches that sought the apostle's ministry
played a significant part in determining the places where Paul and his fellow-
workers labor (Philippians 2:12, 19-25; 2 Corinthians 1:15-23);" (Edmund
P. Clowney, *Called to the Ministry* [Chicago: Inter-Varsity, 1964], p. 87).

ous crisis in the life of a church. In other crises the church has pastoral guidance. Why is it that in calling a pastor, too many churches fail to obtain professional assistance? There is probably no other person who knows the potential candidate better than does his district superintendent, especially if he has held this position for some time. It is tragic that some churches shy from denominational assistance because of a fear of denominational control. The denomination, however, is no stronger than its local churches, and thus certainly has a priority concern for the local congregation. No church is required to follow the suggestions from the denomination, but it certainly should consider that advice seriously. The denomination is in the position to know and should be consulted to substantiate or question advice and recommendations received from other sources. More and more churches are recognizing the advantage of such help and are working more closely with denomination leaders in selecting pastors. The results prove worthwhile. Some denominational leaders are so convinced of this that, for example, the Baptist General Conference initiates the contact with a church whose pastor has resigned, and offers help. Not all churches accept such an offer, but most welcome it. A denominational leader can often step into the breach and fulfill the pastoral guidance that a church needs in selecting a pastor. Too many churches have overlooked this valuable assistance.

If, however, the churches are going to seek help from the denomination, then the denomination is obligated to have immediately available current, in-depth information. Of course, gaining such information is dependent upon the cooperation of pastors. But the denomination should have a working system whereby it periodically collects such information about its ministers. Eleven denominations responded to the survey concerning this aspect of their service to local congregations. Eight of the eleven keep an active file on their pastors and make this information available to churches on request.

Ten out of the eleven denominations responding also keep

an active file on each of their churches. This information is available to assist ministers in making meaningful decisions concerning a change in pastorates. Of course these files are only as current and as adequate as the churches make them in responding to annual or periodic requests for information by the denominations.

The denominations which are serious about assisting churches in finding the right pastor should also provide procedural outlines for self-studies and make available a team of churchmen to assist in this study. The denominations should provide printed forms or guideline questions for both church and candidate to submit to one another. If such standard questionnaires are used, no party will feel embarrassed or think that a certain approach or line of questioning is out of order. This results in obtaining sufficient information for an intelligent decision under the direction of the Holy Spirit. Important details will not be missed.

The Interim Pastor

Another consideration related to denominational help is that of providing interim or supply pastors while the church is seeking a new pastor. Traditionally this has been a place for effective ministry by retired men. Interim pastors can also be secured from college and seminary faculties and student bodies. Occasionally men from a denominational head-quarter's staff are available. One denomination has two men engaged in this work full time. One is not retired, but is in his forties. He is a bachelor and therefore does not have immediate family responsibilities. His ministry meets a very vital need. The survey of pastors and churches indicates that the majority would appreciate the denomination providing supply or interim pastors, especially if the church finds itself without a pastor for an extended period of time. When making the initial contact with the denomination for assistance, a church may want to inquire as to whether such provisions are available to the church. The Pacific Northwest District of the Evangelical Free Church has a number of interim pastors available. This has been most helpful to the churches of that district.

A period of time with an interim pastor may be helpful to the church. He is usually a man of experience. Nevertheless, the employing of such should be carefully thought out and all agreements fully understood by both the church and the supply pastor. Usually the arrangements are for a stated period of time, at the end of which there is automatic termination. If the period is not stated, the arrangement may be terminated at any time by either the minister or the church. This should be fully understood by the pastor and the church. Such an understanding relieves certain tensions and eliminates some possible undercurrent. It should also be understood that the interim pastor will stay out of the way of the pulpit committee. He should not meet with them unless they invite him to do so. Even then, his advice should be of a general nature. He should not champion for a particular minister, as if he had a special "in with God" concerning His man for the church. His association with the church, however, may give him certain insights which, coupled with possible knowledge about particular ministers, may provide helpful suggestions when asked for.

The appointment of an interim pastor may be of special value in particular cases. For example, if the former pastor has been an unusually dynamic, charismatic type individual, a break before a new pastor is appointed may be wise. Without it the next pastorate may be brief, or at best more stormy than necessary, especially during the early months. When there has been an unhappy situation in the church and the pastor has left under duress, a carefully chosen interim pastor (a man of experience, maturity, and love) may help heal the wound and strengthen the church. Such an interim pastor should be told something of the problem so he can courageously and lovingly deal with it.

Sometimes a pastor is taken by death, or for some reason

does not give adequate notice. The church needs time to adjust and seek a new pastor. An interim pastor may be the answer in such cases. He will be able to give continuity to the pulpit ministry and prevent a hodgepodge of preaching or repetitions which often happens with a long variety of pulpit supplies. When an interim pastor is on the scene, certain factions in the church will be discouraged from maneuvering to obtain their favorite preacher to emphasize a particular doctrine or tangent theological thrust. The financial situation of the church may dictate the need of an interim pastor. This, however, should only be for a stipulated period of time. Whatever the reason for obtaining an interim pastor, his duties must be clearly outlined, and his financial support determined, in a written agreement.

Honest Openness Is the Best Policy

One of the perplexing problems for the church is to know how to react to the knowledge that their pastor is out candidating, or at least looking for another church. The pastor should be openly honest with the officers of the church concerning any candidating plans. He should not attempt to candidate secretly. If the pastor does not take this initiative in an open approach, the church must do so. If "candidating on the sly" by the pastor becomes known to some in the church, the officers should kindly ask for a conference with the pastor in order to understand his feelings and plans. If the deacons or elders believe it is untimely for their pastor to consider a change, they should tell him so. This may be all he needs to reaffirm his call and thus continue in his present ministry with greater fervor. It is not necessary or advisable to involve the whole church in the matter, but open honesty between officers and pastor is always the best policy.

If this practice is maintained, then it is not so difficult to call the pastor into conference when it is agreed by the official board that his resignation would be best for him and for the church. This may seem idealistic, but it has worked and can work if there is mutual faith and trust throughout the years of a pastor-church relationship. One further detail that causes friction at times is the question of who pays for the pulpit supply when the pastor is away candidating. Usually the pastor's present church graciously underwrites this cost, but there must be full understanding by both pastor and church concerning this. In keeping with good church etiquette, the church who requests a pastor to candidate should offer to pay his present church the cost of a pulpit supply during his absence.

SELECT A PULPIT COMMITTEE

When a pastoral change has been agreed upon mutually by church and pastor and his resignation has been accepted, the church's immediate responsibility is to elect a pulpit committee or activate the standing committee. Although the term "pulpit committee" may be a misnomer and would better be the "pastor search committee," the term is so ingrained in church vocabulary there is little hope of changing it.

COMMITTEE REPRESENTATION AND SIZE

It is best not to employ a present board to act as the pulpit committee. It is better practice to carefully select a fresh committee who represent different areas of the church's ministry and embody the best wisdom of the membership. It is not necessary that every organization in the church be represented on the committee, nor should leaders of major organizations be automatically placed on the committee. Members of the pulpit committee should be selected primarily for their spiritual maturity, working knowledge of the Word of God, and understanding of the church universal and the local church in particular. They should be persons of insight and love. The positions they hold in the church organization or government is not the primary concern. It is essential that those on the committee know the church well, or at least take time to know it well. Every member should expect to give of himself sacrificially to the sacred task of the committees' appointment.

How many members should a pulpit committee have? Five members constitutes a good working size. Three is sufficient. Seven or nine should be adequate for any size church. Never have an even number on the committee.

DETERMINE RESPONSIBILITIES AND AUTHORITY

The pulpit committee should have its responsibilties well outlined and its authority well understood. It is difficult for a committee to serve effectively unless the church makes it very clear what is expected of them. There should be a written description of what the pulpit committee is expected to do and what authority it has. Too often the committee oversteps its authority or serves irresponsibly, simply because there is no job description. This only causes dissension and poor relationships between committee and church. Some factors to be understood are:

1. Who outlines the qualifications of the desired pastor? Is a self-study to be made? By whom?
2. What budget does the pulpit committee have to work with, and what accounting of the money is expected by the church?
3. For what length of time is the committee elected?
4. Does the committee's responsibility include supplying the pulpit during the interim period, or is another committee (pulpit supply committee) responsible for that? What coordination do these two committees have so the pulpit committee knows what Sundays are open for possible candidates? Communication between these two committees must be constant so that two men are not scheduled to speak at the same service, or a man being considered by the pulpit committee is not prematurely invited to fill the pulpit.

5. What kind of reports does the church expect from the pulpit committee, and how often?
6. How much autonomy does the committee have in preliminary investigation and careful study before a man is recommended?
7. How much does the church want the pulpit committee to communicate to a serious candidate concerning salary and related financial considerations?

Calvary Temple of Hartford, Connecticut, outlined the functions of their pulpit committee as follows:

1. Determine selection of reputable sources and develop means for contact to obtain candidate recommendations.
2. Coordinate all information relating to prospective candidates and maintain a record of such material.
3. Establish criteria for evaluation of prospects and conduct preliminary screening for selection of the most qualified candidates.
4. Arrange for such additional investigations, as necessary, including visitation to other churches, to permit selection of candidates who should receive an official letter of inquiry. (Note: The committee will consider one prime candidate at a time, and only when the disposition has been completed, will it proceed with another candidate.)
5. Maintain liaison with Executive Committee, reporting progress and advising the Chairman of the Deacons of candidate visitation dates for coordination of pulpit supply schedule.
6. Handle travel and hospitality arrangements for candidates scheduled to preach in our church. As circumstances permit, the Pulpit Committee shall also arrange for an informal reception, open to the Executive Committee and the honorary deacons, to provide an opportunity for a friendly exchange of information with the candidate.

It is not the responsibility of this committee to *name* a

pastor for the church. Its purpose is to *recommend* a pastor.
The church in the final analysis, may either accept or reject
the recommendation.‡ The pulpit committee simply makes
possible a more orderly and efficient method of securing a
pastor. The work of the church should be done decently and
in order. (1 Co 14:40).

As soon as the committee is named or activated it should
begin immediately to consider prayerfully and carefully its
task. Some churches feel they show disrespect to their present
pastor by considering the mechanics of obtaining a new
pastor while he is still on the field. This idea must be dismissed for the good of the church. A pastor whose heart is
for the future of his church will welcome and appreciate the
activating of a pulpit committee directly after his resignation,
even to the extent of vacating his pulpit for a possible candidate. If there has been, and continues to be, a good spirit
between pastor and people, this procedure holds no embarrassment or problem.

The church must face seriously its responsibilities during
the interim period without a pastor. It is possible for a church
to grow spiritually and even numerically while without a
pastor. Everything possible must be done to keep good relationships between the pulpit committee and the rest of the
church. Defining the committee's responsibilities and authority as suggested above will assist in this greatly. Reports
should be received regularly from the committee. Pastoral
responsibilities will have to be delegated to deacons and other
church leaders. This must not be part of the pulpit committee's job. They have enough to do. The official board should
handle these concerns and any administrating problems. An

‡"It is possible for a church to disregard any recommendation of its pulpit
committee, and in a few rare cases this may be wise, but ordinarily a church
will want to follow the recommendation of its pulpit committee, and wisely
so" (Clarence E. Colton, *The Minister's Mission* [Dallas: Story Book Press,
1951], p. 43).

"While a church may intrust the matter of securing a pastor to a representative committee, the report of such a committee need not be regarded
as final" (Charles R. Erdman, *The Work of the Pastor* [Philadelphia: Westminster, 1924], pp. 13-14).

interim pastor may be needed, and the pulpit committee should probably be given the responsibility of securing this man. They will have the information and necessary resources.

Because of lesser salary expenses during the interim period, the wise church will establish a contingency fund for expenses incurred in moving the new pastor and renovating the parsonage and study.

UTILIZE ADVANTAGES

As strange as it may sound at first, there are certain advantages to being without a pastor for a period of time. The church leaders must capitalize on these advantages. Without a pastor, members may more quickly sense a personal responsibility for the work of the church and give themselves more fully in service for Christ. The work may not go as smoothly, but members may be less demanding and more sympathetic, and thus more easily may overlook mistakes. This can result in certain persons overcoming their previous critical, complaining spirit. With a mutual concern in determining God's choice for their pastor, members may take time to think and pray more carefully concerning the type of man the church really needs. This should cause members to evaluate their church more objectively to determine the qualifications of a future pastor. The result will be a better understanding of their church. Certainly the struggle that the church mutually shares during this interim will cause many members to appreciate the new pastor as he takes on responsibilities that they have shouldered. In fact, the new pastor may find some of the congregation more ready to give needed assistance because of the experiential understanding of the pastor's work.

The attitude of the church during the time without a pastor should be to face the problems realistically and take advantage of the benefits that period can provide.

THE CHURCH VOTE

When a candidate has been thoroughly investigated, has

been heard by the people, and is to be voted on by the church, what is the best policy in regard to the vote and its report to the candidate? The vote must be by ballot, with no absentee ballots allowed from nonresident members. These two rules are basic safeguards. The ballot vote gives each member opportunity to express his decision on the matter, without the embarrassment of being identified if he honestly must vote in the minority. Most constitutions call for a ballot vote on all important matters, and wisely so. Not allowing absentee ballots from nonresident members also protects the church against outside pressure. How can a nonresident member vote intelligently on a man he has never met or heard? The practice of some churches is to take a second ballot when the negative votes include only a very small minority in order to make the call unanimous. There is really no benefit in this practice. The second ballot has not really changed the minds of people. It has only led them to resign themselves to the situation because they are outnumbered and thus feel pressured to change their votes. The better policy is to take the first ballot count and report it to the candidate as is.

The exact count should be sent to the candidate as part of his letter of call. This starts the relationship on a sound and honest basis. Wayland once said, "I don't think much of these unanimous calls. It looks as though people did not judge for themselves."[8]

The Annual Call

Although only indirectly related to the candidating procedure, some comments should be made on the habit of some churches who, by vote, give their pastor an annual call. At one time, this policy may have been a valid protective device, as seen in the following study. However, the policy has outlived its usefulness. In the early days of New England the minister was commonly settled for life. He expected to spend all of his useful life with the church where he was first settled. Sometimes he even gave to that church a bond as surety for the due fulfillment of his duties. Legally he had a life tenure there. He could not be dismissed unless convicted of one or more of three "crimes": (1) if he preached and departed from the essential doctrines of the church, (2) if he were willfully negligent of his duties, or (3) if he were guilty of immoral or criminal conduct. Such a minister could fight the accusation if he chose to and his church was then obliged to take the case before an ecclesiastical council or court of law. Until he was duly dismissed, the church was obliged to pay his salary, and its property could be attached and levied upon by law for this purpose.[9]

A series of rather important legal decisions in Massachusetts courts during the first half of the nineteenth century strongly supported the principle of the minister's right to life tenure when no provision was made in the call for some method to dissolve the church-pastoral relationship. The courts seem to have thought that security of tenure was essential to the dignity and effectiveness of the minister's work. Perhaps it was as a result of these decisions that some churches, desiring to safeguard themselves from some known or experienced unhappy situation, adopted the custom of inserting in the call a provision for termination. As some churches broke from the state church, no doubt such measures were included in their policies even to the extent of the "annual call." This also may be the reason why early in American Christianity the tradition of the short pastorate developed within the non-state churches:

> Common observation seemed to indicate that the preacher's richest evangelistic results came during his first and second years in a pastorate; that his zeal and popularity tended to decline during his third year, and that by the end of his fourth year he needed a new field and the church a new pastor. In order to keep church and pastor from growing static, one great denomination established a normal four-year limit. Churches electing the pastors generally fell in with this tradition and built up the expectation of frequent change

of pastors. Among many churches the custom of the "annual call" arose, probably as a protective measure in order to in- sure a church against embarrassment in terminating the serv- ice of an undesirable preacher.[10]

Whatever the reason for its use or adoption, the policy certainly is not based on mutual Christian faith and respect. It is an escape from having to face squarely the concern of pastoral change with honest openness which is always the best for both pastor and church. Essentially this policy can- not be too strongly deprecated. It is either a very disconcert- ing annual encounter, or it becomes a rather humorous tra- dition, or an opportunity for the dictatorial pastor to identify his enemies and become stronger. None of these can justify its use.

The annual call or resignation has many built-in problems. Pattison calls it a vicious plan. It places the minister in a position no more secure than that of a stated supply pastor. He is too much at the mercy of any dissatisfied clique. It certainly is not a plan conducive to the best interests of the church, when every year it has the unsettling experience of discussing whether the minister shall or shall not continue for another year. It discourages long-range planning. It provides an easy escape from facing problems honestly and openly, and an uncertain hope that a pastoral change will somehow mysteriously provide the panacea.

> It degrades the pastoral office, hampers the minister's success and almost forces his work into perfunctory molds such as no minister should tolerate. Moreover, it places him at the mercy of every grumbler in the parish, inviting them once a year to gather in force for his discomfiture. So sacred a re- lationship as that which binds pastor and people cannot stand the chill of a too commercial atmosphere. Neither the church nor the minister will prosper and be in harmony when the pecuniary question is forced to the front. This is a practice to which no minister who respects himself ought to submit.[11]

No church should force such a situation upon its pastor. There would be no need for such a policy if church and pastor would keep the communication lines open as Christian brothers should. The practice of an annual call cannot be recommended.

THE ESSENTIAL OF PRAYER

The final guidelines for the church are surely the most important. The church must call itself to fervent and faithful prayer. Reports from the pulpit committee should be distributed to keep each organization informed as to its progress, and to provide "prayer fuel" for the people. No organization should meet without special prayer to God for the selection of His man for the church. Deacons and other officers should meet regularly for prayer. Special prayer meetings should be called, with prayer groups in homes meeting periodically. So important is the choice of a pastor that some churches encourage fasting with prayer—waiting on God expectantly. Choosing a pastor should be an exercise in holiness! In and through all the suggestions given in this book, the overshadowing priority is that the Holy Spirit must lead the way.

LEADING OF THE HOLY SPIRIT

In every step taken, the leading of the Holy Spirit is essential. From the survey, however, some apparently feel that the Holy Spirit has no need of facts and that a thorough investigation indicates a lack of dependence upon God. All that is needed, they say, is a season of prayer until God's Spirit makes it plain whom He wants. They seem to believe that gathering information is helpful, not in selecting the man, but only in letting him know what he is getting into, and telling the church what to expect. Some who answered the questionnaire chided the author concerning this point. One said, "It seems you have left out the most important aspect of all—that of the church being led by the Holy Spirit and the man of God being genuinely led of the Holy Spirit in knowing deep in his heart that this is of the Lord." Another stated, "It seems that something of the utmost importance has been deleted in this questionnaire: that is the Holy Spirit in the call. Personally I would not leave a church because of any other reason than that I felt the Holy Spirit was leading me to go: nor would I accept an invitation to candidate at a church unless I felt the Lord was directing that way . . . The other things are incidental."

These men missed a key question of the survey that indicated how information and facts are instruments by which the Holy Spirit reveals the will of God. The guidelines mentioned in this book are simply that—instruments which may be used by the Holy Spirit in leading churches to pastors, and pastors to churches. One pastor said, "God by His Holy Spirit uses people; their heads, hearts, eyes, ears and that inner sense to point to the proper 'fit'—man to church. Therefore the more exposure on every level possible, the more completely God can guide." This is certainly the way the Holy Spirit led in giving us the Bible. If we make a decision on the basis of feeling alone, we lay ourselves open to great delusions. One cannot separate the leading of the Holy Spirit from careful investigation. The one does not preclude the other. They work hand in hand. The Holy Spirit places no premium on ignorance.

Summary

There are many considerations for the church to face. The church must recognize the innate problems of basing its decision for a pastor on the hearing of one or two sermons. It must dismiss from its mind the idea of "hiring" a minister. Concern for and courtesy to sister churches must be brought into play. Understanding its own needs should be the basis for considering the qualities desired in the selection of a pastor. Denominational help should not be minimized, but utilized, and the possibility of employing an interim pastor should be considered. Open honesty is the best policy for pastor-church relationships. This same policy should be followed by a pulpit committee that is wisely chosen by the church.

The attitude of the church during the time without a pastor should be to face the problems realistically and take advantage of the benefits which that period can provide. Careful, businesslike procedures bathed in much prayer should govern the actual business meeting when the vote is taken on the candidate. The practice of subjecting the pastor to the rigors of an annual call should be discontinued. The church in dependence upon the Holy Spirit, must immerse itself in much prayer for God to give His wisdom and leading through the whole procedure of selecting a new pastor. It is not enough to say that the Holy Spirit will lead the right man to the right church. The survey of pastors and churches strongly emphasizes that God's will must be sufficiently sought before it is found.§

The Holy Spirit puts no premium on ignorance. He does not ordinarily guide a church to the right pastor through a supernatural disclosure. "More often divine guidance is given through the available channels of prayer, investigation, conference and discussion, reasoning, conclusions based on sound judgment, and confirmation by vote of a praying people."[12]

---

§Does careful screening of a possible candidate and careful investigation of a church by a candidate indicate a lack of faith on the part of the church or ministry? Of the 558 persons who answered this question on the survey, 10 answered yes and 548 answered no.

4

Organization and Philosophy of the Pulpit Committee

FORMATION OF THE PULPIT COMMITTEE

Some churches have a standing pulpit committee which has responsibilities other than that of searching for a pastor when the position is vacated. Most churches appoint a new committee each time this need arises. This is the better procedure. How is this done? The tradition or constitution of the church often dictates the procedure. The committee is usually nominated by the deacons, nominating committee, or church council. The church then elects a committee, preferably by ballot. If there is no constitutional or traditional method for nominating a committee, the church may, after determining the number to be on the committee, have its members list their choices by secret ballot.

Double the number to be on the committee, and that number of persons most listed becomes the nominees. The church then votes for the committee from this list by secret ballot. For example, if a seven-member committee is desired, take the fourteen names listed most often and have the church members vote for seven of them. This is a quick method, but it may not result in the quality committee that a careful nominating committee would recommend. Careful work by a nominating committee should result in a more adequate pulpit committee composed of spiritually mature and thoughtful church members who have the interest of the total church at heart and who are above promoting personal prejudice or desire. The committee should be representative of the church, including age span. It should not be some existing committee saddled with the new responsibility of finding a pastor.

How many members should the committee have? Three or five can easily work and travel together, and attend meetings with a minimum of conflicts. Every person has many ideas, desires, and emotions. The more people who serve on the committee, the greater the possibility of misinterpretation and turmoil.

The concept of additive and non-additive relationships may also be considered here. The following chart explains the importance of this.

Committee of three $= a+b+c =$ 6 relationships
(ab, ac, ba, bc, ca, cb)
Committee of four $=$ 18 relationships
Committee of five $=$ 44 relationships
Committee of six $=$ 100 relationships
Committee of seven $=$ 222 relationships
Committee of eight $=$ 490 relationships
Committee of nine $=$ 1,080 relationships[1]

Both concepts mentioned above, the plurality within one individual and the increasing ratio of interpersonal relationships to the number in the group, emphasize the importance of keeping a pulpit committee relatively small. The point is that a small, well-chosen and representative committee will act more efficiently than a large one.

If, however, a church feels that its pulpit committee must be large, it should appoint an executive committee, consisting of the chairman, secretary, and one other, authorized to conduct negotiations without being obliged to call the whole committee together for every detail. This executive committee may be given the responsibility to do some initial scouting for a pastor.

Because pulpit committees are often composed of older people, there may be a tendency to recruit a pastor primarily to please the older people, who in the course of a few years will either die or be incapacitated. The danger of this tendency is obvious. The better plan is to have youth and young adults represented on the committee. In particular, those under forty-five should be more largely represented than those above that age, since upon them will lie the responsibility for the church during the next twenty-five years. Chronological age must not be the only criteria, for such does not always designate a mature person. Some men are more hopelessly set and nonprogressive at thirty than others are at sixty.

The suggested maximum number for the pulpit committee is nine. One person may be able to represent more than one area of the church's ministry. "The committee must not be too large, else it will be unwieldy; it must not be too small, else it will be unrepresentative. With utmost care the church should select a committee that will fairly represent all the age groups and activities of the church. One question should be uppermost: How to find the will of God in the interests of our church and the causes it represents?"[2]

Term of the Pulpit Committee

If the pulpit committee is chosen prayerfully and carefully it should be able to accomplish its task within a year's time. Because certain "power strata" may make it difficult for an adequately representative committee to be formed, some provision to terminate the committee should be made. A recommendation is that the committee be elected for a specific duration of time. One year is suggested. Some pulpit committees have been known to drag their feet and operate with diminishing returns. The longer they work, the slower they work. The longer a church is without a pastor, the more difficult it is to obtain one. Pastors contacted often conclude that it is a troubled church that has difficulty in obtaining a pastor. If the church elects the committee for one year, it does have the privilege to appoint a different committee at the end of that time, or at least to pump new blood into it if the situation indicates. If, on the other hand, the committee is hard at work and evidences good potential, it may be reelected for another year or six months.

INNER ORGANIZATION OF THE COMMITTEE

First a chairman is named. This may be done by the church when the committee is elected, or left to the committee at its first meeting. The chairman is the spokesman for the committee. To avoid possible confusion all contacts with candidates should be made or approved by him. A vice-chairman should be selected to act in the absence of the chairman and upon special instructions by the committee. The secretarial position is a responsible one, for he records and preserves the records of meetings, discussions, decisions, and recommendations. The collating and filing of information also falls within this person's duties, and therefore he may need an assigned assistant. A time and place for holding regular meetings is agreed on by the committee.

DETERMINING A PHILOSOPHY AND PROCEDURE

The church seeking a pastor must establish a clearly defined philosophy and procedure for inviting a candidate to its pulpit. One pastor received a "feeler" from a particular church, then immediately went on vacation, but left the letter at home. While on vacation he answered the letter, but mistakenly sent it to another church of a similar name in the same town. He received a reply from that church thanking him for his prompt reply. That church, too, was looking for a pastor, but apparently did not keep a record of those to whom they sent letters of inquiry. In another situation, a pastor candidated on a Sunday, but was informed upon arrival that a call had been extended and accepted by another minister the previous Wednesday. He had traveled 400 miles by train and 150 miles by bus. The church bulletin informed still another pastor that a certain minister had already accepted the call to the church where he had come to candidate. The chairman of one small church kindly informed the supposed candidate, just before he was to speak on Sunday morning, that the church had already called a pastor. A student at a seminary and his dorm-mate both received calls to the same church. Once, a minister was actually called at the conclusion of the candidating service, at a business meeting held in his presence. Obviously he received a unanimous call.

Because of inadequate screening before congregational approval, one church narrowly missed (by a few votes) engaging a man who had left his previous residence with many unpaid bills. A pastor who left one church came at his own request and preached in a church which needed a pastor. He made a big impression and was called, although the church knew nothing of his record. In six months he left. One pastor was asked to candidate at a church, but refused to do so when he learned the church planned to hear six candidates before voting. A district superintendent overheard a parishioner say, "I'm certainly not going to vote for the first man who candidates." These sad incidents point up the dire need for careful procedural planning on the part of the church and its pulpit committee.

AUTHORITY, LIMITATIONS AND RESPONSIBILITIES OF THE COMMITTEE

Every church constitution should not only outline the procedure for formulating a pulpit committee but also determine its authority, limitations, and responsibilities. The carefully chosen committee should have certain guidelines, and should be given authority to speak on behalf of the church. Ideally, the pulpit committee should be allowed and encouraged to mention specific needs, qualifications, and financial arrangements. The more definite the committee can be, the more efficient its work will be. Too detailed an outline of responsibilities, however, may restrict the committee and hamper its efficiency and productivity. In financial matters the pulpit committee should be allowed to negotiate at least between a high and low figure, depending on the minister's experience and training. If the church fails to outline the committee's responsibilities, the committee itself should draw up plans for their work and ask the church for approval. Procedure without a mutually agreed-upon plan can result in poor pulpit committee-church relations. (See pp. 40-41.)

UNITY AND CONFIDENTIALITY

One of the two most important characteristics of the pulpit committee is *unity*. Work cannot go forward without unity. Prayer and mutual support will enhance this. It must be understood that theirs is a team endeavor, with no superstar calling the signals. *Confidentiality* is the second essential ingredient of the committee. There must be a covenanted promise to keep all reports and files on pastors and churches confidential. Too many pastors have had their reputations tarnished by some careless committee member sharing confidential information. Only when it is agreed by the committee shall a name even be mentioned to the church. News travels rapidly. If a church hears that their pastor is being considered by another church, they may wrongly conclude that he wants to leave, and the church is thrown into needless turmoil. Committee members must agree to keep confidential the names they consider.

CAREFUL AND THOROUGH INVESTIGATION

The overall rule for the pulpit committee is that the procedure involve careful and full investigation. Again, the survey indicated that churches and pastors definitely feel that a candidate should be just as carefully investigated as a potential executive is by a business firm considering him for a salaried position.* One pastor commented that most churches could not afford this in-depth investigation. Most churches, however, can ill afford not to.

During a conversation one minister mentioned that he had interacted with six pulpit committees (he was ready to move to his third pastorate), and not one of them had asked him a question about his doctrinal position. Another pastor reported that a church where he was candidating inquired about his wife's musical ability, but never questioned him about his doctrinal beliefs. Still another candidate was asked nothing as to experience, doctrinal view, or past ministries. The result was chaos. One woman voted for a candidate because he had such pretty white hair. In another church a man was heard to say, "I knew that he was the man as soon as his wife played the piano." In a recent survey of nearly 2,000 Southern Baptist Churches, two out of ten churches said that when they called their pastor they did not know how much experience he had, what he believed, and what preaching ability he had. More than one-half of the churches did not know about the man's conversion experience, his family, whether he paid his debts, or could control his temper.[3] Yet the Scripture indicates that certain qualifications must be met by pastors of churches.

NEW TESTAMENT STANDARDS FOR PASTORS

The pulpit committee should have a standard and know what kind of pastor they are looking for. New Testament qualifications have been well outlined by Hill.[4]

OUTWARD REPUTATION

Have a good reputation even when his life is lived as an open book (1 Ti 3:2; Titus 1:7).

Be well thought of, even by those outside the church (1 Ti 3:7).

---

*Should a possible candidate be investigated as carefully as a business investigates a potential executive? Of the 530 persons answering this question, 470 said yes and 60 said no.

Be irreproachable in his marital relations (1 Ti 3:2; Titus 1:6).

In other words, a pastor is to be a man who has a good reputation in his church, in society, and in his home.

INNER DISPOSITION

Not selfish, quick-tempered, intemperate, violent, or overly interested in material things (1 Ti 3:3; Titus 1:7).

Have a love for people and for that which is good (1 Ti 3:2; Titus 1:8).

Be sensible, mature, well-balanced, and self-controlled (1 Ti 3:2; Titus 1:8).

Be Christlike and devoted to God (Titus 1:8).

A pastor with the right kind of inner disposition should have right attitudes toward himself and toward God, and should reflect Christian maturity.

CHRISTIAN EXPERIENCE

Not a novice or new convert (1 Ti 3:6).

Prove himself faithful and able to guide others by managing his own household well; should have believing and obedient children (1 Ti 3:4; Titus 1:6).

Be a skillful teacher (1 Ti 3:2), one who has been taught what is true and knows how to teach it to others (Titus 1:9).

ONE CANDIDATE AT A TIME

Once a standard is determined and self-study has indicated the specific·qualifications needed in a pastor, a policy of procedure must be agreed upon. The method least acceptable is for the committee to hear many candidates through a long succession of Sundays. This method includes the distasteful competitive element and odious comparisons. It usually results in confusion and splitting the committee, if not the church, into opposing factions. One church heard six candidates in a row and tried to decide between them. They finally settled on two, but had to call them back for a rerun. Another church stated that they voted on three candidates at one time and just could not decide. One pastor candidated in a church, not knowing they already had another candidate the Sunday before. When the vote was taken, the congregation was evenly divided between the two.

No author consulted in this study suggested, not a single pastor indicated, and not even one denominational leader agreed that two or more candidates should be considered at the same time. Of all suggestions by those with experience and knowledge, not one was more emphasized than that the church should consider *one candidate at a time.*

One of the denominational leaders who agreed that two candidates should never be considered together warned, nevertheless, about a possible misunderstanding on this policy. He stated that this does not mean for the pulpit committee to become inoperative the moment it agrees to have a candidate come to the church for interviews and to preach. Even if the man is eventually presented to the church for a vote, the committee should not unintentionally indicate to the church by lax effort or attitude that this is the only man available. The pulpit committee must anticipate that the church may reject their recommendation and thus constantly keep working so that when a man is ready to be presented to the church for a vote the comment from the committee can be, "We have a number of men under investigation, but we feel that this one is worthy of serious consideration and would like to submit his name for a vote." This prevents the church from feeling pressured to vote "yes" or else to be without a pastor for a length of time because no other prospects are in sight.

INVESTIGATE FIRST—CANDIDATE LAST

We have attempted to show that much more information must be gained about a possible pastor than what is available in hearing one or two sermons. In fact, gathering much of this information must be done before deciding to invite the man to candidate. Otherwise the invitation is done ignorantly and can be a waste of the church's money and time—to say nothing of the pastor's valuable time and the unnecessary upset such an invitation may cause the minister's present church. Any church can discover whether a man is qualified to serve as their pastor after he becomes their pastor—but that is much too late if he proves to be inadequate or unqualified.

More than one pulpit committee has found itself in an embarrassing situation because it waited until after the church heard a man preach before checking his qualifications. To learn as much as possible about a prospective pastor in advance of asking him to candidate, and certainly in advance of calling him, is not an optional matter for the church. A pastor must meet the qualifications for pastors listed in 1 Timothy 3:1-7 and Titus 1:6-9. Careful investigation is essential. Lloyd Perry puts it succinctly: "Investigate the pastor fully before asking him to candidate."[5] Similarly, Foote says, "This investigation . . . should be made before, and not after, the men under consideration are invited to preach."[6]

SUMMARY

The pulpit committee carries heavy and varied responsibilities. The church is responsible for the careful formation of a committee that is small enough to work efficiently, but large enough to be representative. The term of the committee and its inner organization must be determined along with a basic philosophy and workable procedure. Careful investigation must be made of men seriously considered on the basis of the New Testament standard for pastors. The committee is to investigate thoroughly before suggesting the candidate. The committee must never recommend two or more candidates to the church at one time. Unity and confidentiality are the two essential characteristics of the working committee.

5

Duties of the Pulpit Committee

Once the pulpit committee has been organized and its philosophy of operation determined, it must concern itself immediately with certain priority considerations.

CHOOSE AN INTERIM PASTOR

If the situation indicates the necessity, the church may request the pulpit committee to secure an interim pastor. The provision of an interim pastor will allow for the work of the pulpit committee to be less hurried and for the work of the church to move more efficiently. The district superintendent and/or denominational leader can assist the church in securing such a man. The basic rule is that no interim pastor or pulpit supply speaker is eligible for consideration as a prospective pastor. This should be the understanding when he is asked to come. Much possible misunderstanding and friction can be avoided by this agreement.* The result of the survey questionnaire indicates that churches, pastors, and district superintendents feel strongly that securing an interim pastor

*Although this is the strong advice of denominational leaders, many churches and pastors indicated from the survey that the possibility of the interim pastor being considered as a candidate should be allowed. Of the 226 local church officers who answered this question, 190 felt that the interim pastor could be considered for the pastoral position. Thirty-six indicated that he should not be so considered. Of the 302 pastors answering this question, 144 checked yes that the interim pastor could be considered for the pastoral position, and fifty-eight said no.

should be seriously considered by pastorless churches.† One word of caution may need to be given the pulpit committee in regard to an interim pastor. A fine interim pastor may tempt the pulpit committee to become apathetic toward its responsibilities. Too much delay may discourage a church, so the duration of the interim pastor's ministry should be designated in advance. Three to six months is an acceptable arrangement, with a year being the maximum time for an interim ministry. When the situation indicates the need of an interim pastor and the pulpit committee has a man to recommend, the usual procedure of ballot vote by the church should be followed. Another possibility is for the pulpit committee to be authorized by the church to obtain and employ an interim pastor for a specific length of time.

IDENTIFYING NEEDS AND DETERMINING PASTORAL QUALIFICATIONS

It has already been suggested that a brief self-study of the church be undertaken as soon as a pastoral resignation is accepted. The next few pages of this chapter and appendix A provide some guidelines for this study. The entire need of the church must be carefully considered and every age included in the analysis. It is often difficult for church members and officers to do this job objectively; thus it may be very profitable for the pulpit committee to have some assistance in this study from Christian education experts, a district superintendent and/or a mature, experienced pastor. It may be possible for the departing pastor to assist. An organization that may be of some assistance to a church doing a self-study is the Associated Church Builders, Inc., Box 187, Palatine,

†Four hundred fifty-two persons said that an interim pastor gives stability to the church during the time seeking a new pastor. Three hundred twenty-five said that such gave more time to investigate and secure a pastor. Three hundred sixty-eight indicated that the interim pastor should be employed when there is difficulty in finding a pastor and the church shows signs of deterioration. Only six indicated that none of the above three reasons justified the employment of an interim pastor and sixty-nine said that interim pastors should be considered only in very exceptional cases. Not one of these was a district superintendent.

Illinois, 60067. Although this group's feasibility study is geared to a building program, there are many facets that would assist the pulpit committee. From this study the priority needs can be determined, and from this listing the type of pastor to be recruited will be indicated.

One pastor wisely commented that he observes the needs of the church extending him an invitation to candidate and compares these with his own strong points. Another pastor said, "I would expect a pulpit committee to have considered the type of man needed for the church and then proceed to find a man best qualified for their situation." These statements succinctly point to the value of a church self-study.

MAKE A CHURCH SELF-STUDY

Part of the procedural policy of the pulpit committee should include the gathering of sufficient, up-to-date information about its own church so that intelligent interaction can be had with the pastor when he asks questions about the church. How much should a pulpit committee know about its own church? As much as possible! The self-study will provide much of this needed information. The first area of consideration is to determine the philosophy of the local church. This is most essential. If the church cannot agree on its purpose, all the rest of the self-study will be quite meaningless. Gathering of information must have a framework for its utilization, otherwise it is just so much data. Without a philosophy, the church cannot intelligently look for a pastor. The search and selection becomes a "hope for the best" endeavor. Once the philosophy has been determined and the self-study completed a basic profile of the pastor needed comes into view. For example, if the local church concludes that it is a "soul saving station," then that church will look for a pastor with the gift of evangelism. It would be unwise to call a man who is committed to the philosophy that the church is primarily a place for training and equipping the saints. Making the self-study may need some objective outside help from church leaders with experience. It is something that needs to be done quite often so the local congregation does not lose sight of its reason for existence and drop into a perfunctory program.

The following is a modification of a suggested list of information areas provided for pulpit committees by Leonard Hill.[1] (See Appendix A for a suggested church self-study procedural form.)

1. PHILOSOPHY

   a. What is the church?
   b. Why does this local church exist?

2. HISTORY

   a. Brief summary of origin and development
   b. Factors affecting growth
   c. General description of the work of former pastors and their lengths of service

3. STATISTICS

   a. Membership: resident and nonresident
   b. Average attendance at all services
   c. Growth trends
   d. Enrollment and average attendance of all organizations
   e. Annual budget with items listed in detail
   f. Financial report showing actual income and expenditures, total gifts to missions and otherwise
   g. Amount and distribution of present debt; how it is financed
   h. Percentage of increase or decrease in attendance and offerings over the past few years

4. PHYSICAL PROPERTY

   a. Property limitations and possibilities for future expansion, including any plans now contemplated

   b. Present situation and problems giving size and arrangement of buildings
   c. Parking facilities: Are they adequate? Future plans?
   d. Parsonage description

5. ORGANIZATION AND OBJECTIVES

   a. List and description of all church organizations and committees; explanation of how they are financed, staffed, and related to one another
   b. List of paid church staff, including job descriptions and relationship to pastor
   c. Comparison of number of volunteer workers to number of jobs to be filled
   d. Church calendar, including long-range plans adopted or under consideration

6. DESCRIPTION OF MEMBERSHIP

   a. Size and special needs of various age groups
   b. Occupations, education, income brackets, interests of members
   c. Number of tithers
   d. Persons active in witnessing
   e. Leadership abilities of membership

7. DESCRIPTION OF COMMUNITY

   a. Population; whether growing, declining, or static
   b. Rural or urban; downtown, residential or in transition
   c. Sources of income; stable or seasonal
   d. Cost of living
   e. Schools and the state ratings
   f. Listing and brief description of all other churches in the community or area
   g. Number of unchurched
   h. Extent of territory from which church draws its members and in which it has an influence
   i. Any exceptional changes: businesses expected to move

in or out, expand or decline; new highways, urban renewal plans, etc.

8. ATTITUDES OF CHURCH MEMBERS

   a. Interest in evangelism, missions, stewardship
   b. Outlook on expansion of building, church staff, or church organizations
   c. Willingness to cooperate with other churches of the denomination and with denominational programs
   d. Attitude and current policy on cooperating with other churches of the community or area
   e. Factors tending to weaken or strengthen the church fellowship and unity
   f. Whether progressive in spirit or slow to accept changes
   g. Customs peculiar to the church or community
   h. What the members expect of a pastor, his wife, his family

9. PROVISIONS FOR PASTOR

   a. Whether called for definite or indefinite period of time
   b. Salary and plan for periodic increases
   c. Amount for moving expenses
   d. Participation in retirement plan
   e. Allowances for car, books, telephone, convention travel, etc.
   f. Length of vacation
   g. Time allowed for speaking engagements
   h. Provision for time off during weekly schedule
   i. Provision for a home; policy on payment of utilities
   j. Time allowed for schooling or secular work
   k. Policy for securing and paying pulpit supplies and special speakers
   l. What agreements are to be in writing; what ones are to be voted on by the church

Not all churches will find all the above relevant to their situation, and other churches will want to add other factors.

Nevertheless, information should be gathered and analyzed just as objectively and honestly as possible. It should tell the whole story—the good and the bad. (See appendix C for sample church information brochures.) The committee must never maneuver or manipulate facts in order to cover up or give a more positive picture:

> A certain church called a minister to its pulpit. He refused to come unless an indebtedness of $10,000 was paid off. The parish committee sent him word that the debt had been taken care of, whereupon he accepted and was duly installed. Then he discovered that ten men in the church had each paid off at the bank $1,000 of the debt, themselves taking notes from the church, so that the church was still in debt, though to its own members instead of to a bank. It is unnecessary to point out that the proceeding was a thoroughly dishonorable deception of the candidate.[2]

The candidate is entitled to full and exact information as to the actual condition of the church, financial and otherwise. A pulpit committee should not expect a minister to respond to a call without adequate knowledge as to his responsibilities and obligations. One young man received a telegram from a very large and wealthy church in Canada asking him to be their youth pastor, but stating nothing more. Apparently they thought their prestige was sufficient for any minister to desire to be a member of its staff. This young man wisely wired back that he was not available. No minister should consider a place of service on such a basis, with no information as to the particulars of the call. There must be a mutual sharing of full information so intelligent decisions can be made by both the minister and the church.

The pulpit committee should never conceal unpleasant facts or discouraging features from the candidate. The survey of churches and pastors indicates that under normal conditions this should be the rule.‡ Some modified this, feeling

‡Do you feel that the church should at times withhold certain information from the candidating minister? Of the 519 persons answering, 124 said yes and 395 said no.

that if past problems have been taken care of and would not affect the future ministry of the church, it is of no value to "hang out the dirty wash." It is certainly not necessary to go into details of old scandals or church squabbles if they do not affect the existing situation.

PASTORAL JOB DESCRIPTION

From this self-study the pulpit committee may draft a job description for the pastor. Not only should the job description reflect these priority needs but also the biblical objectives of the church and the pastoral gifts deemed necessary to the work. The prospective minister certainly has a right to know what the church expects of him. There is no better way to express this in specific terms than through a job description. Every minister has specific objectives which he believes God would have him strive toward in his ministry in relationship to his particular spiritual gifts. He should know if the church's objectives are in line with his objectives, and if the church's specific needs can be met by his specific gifts. The pastor of Glenbard Baptist Church of Glen Ellyn, Illinois, the Reverend Robert Roxburgh, wrote two arresting articles in *Action* magazine some time ago and indicated how successful his job specification idea has been.[3] (Pastor Roxburg's job description is found in Appendix G.)

The job description may be presented to the candidate during preliminary conferences, but it will have greater meaning if given to him during his visit to the church. A job description, without seeing and sensing its context, may convey wrong ideas and/or result in incorrect conclusions. One pastor suggested that the job description be sent to the candidate after the candidating encounter. He will then be able to study it more objectively and to intelligently make a decision by the Holy Spirit if a call is extended to him.

Coupled with this essential to identify the needs and objectives of the church is the necessity to understand the needs of the candidate. Have these needs been identified? Does the support proposed by the church adequately meet these needs?

The pulpit committee must face honestly what common sense should dictate—that not every minister is equally suited to every situation. It is possible for a man to succeed in one field, yet fail in another. The needs of churches and their demands vary greatly. Ministers vary just as much in natural ability, preparation, experience, personality, and insight. One failure should not automatically remove a pastor's name from a list of possible candidates.

The job of the pulpit committee is a very important one, and everyone appointed to it must recognize the seriousness of the committee's responsibilities.

Procedural Considerations

The pulpit committee is now ready to put its philosophy and preliminary planning into active work. They will soon realize that such careful preparation will pay off in efficient productivity as they seriously face a sacred assignment.

DETERMINE SOURCE OF AVAILABLE CANDIDATES

One of the pulpit committee's most important considerations is to determine sources. What men are available, and where can information concerning these men be obtained?

Denominational leaders. If the church officers have not already done so, then certainly one of the first steps for the pulpit committee is to inform the denomination or church fellowship that their particular local congregation is in need of a pastor. The denominational leaders are probably the most important source of information about potential candidates. There is a certain amount of built-in assurance that men recommended by the district superintendents or other denominational leaders will be in line doctrinally with the local church and in sympathy with its basic objectives. These officials usually are in the position to know about available ministers. Often they have seen them in action and are somewhat knowledgeable of their record of performance. Their knowledge of individual churches also enables them to wisely suggest men with abilities suited to particular churches.

Friends and church members. Although suggestions from friends and members of the church are welcome, no great campaign to obtain names should be undertaken. A landslide may ensue, and the inundation may cause much wasted time in digging out. It must be understood, however, that such suggestions will be treated as impartially as an outsider's recommendation. Laymen often have the advantage of having visited other churches while on vacation, or of having been members of churches in other communities, and thus may have some helpful suggestions. When possible, every reasonable suggestion should be investigated so an honest and satisfactory answer can be given to the person who asks about the progress on his suggestion. Often a preliminary letter of inquiry to ministers so recommended quickly eliminates them by their negative response. In the case of a larger church there may be hundreds of names recommended. The committee then must be candid and judicious. From a study of such names, the most likely ones, in the mind of the committee, should be set aside for proper investigation. Reduction of the list of possible candidates to a workable number can be one of the most important concerns that faces the pulpit committee.

Schools. Some seminaries and Bible colleges will assist a church seeking a pastor. Men from their immediate graduating classes who are available may provide the drive and creativity of youth that a particular church needs. Many schools keep active files on their graduates as to their availability for a pastoral change.

Ministers. Although there is a certain amount of clerical loyalty to be considered in the recommendations by fellow pastors, ministers are often valuable sources in finding a pastor. The circumstances govern the wisdom of obtaining recommendations from the resigning pastor and former pastors. Most "pastors of pastors" counsel the resigning minister to keep himself from any relationship with the pulpit committee unless asked, and then his suggestion must never be a personal campaign for a friend. If a former pastor or the resigning pastor is being considered as a possible source, two helpful questions should be asked: Will the church have confidence in the former pastor's recommendation? and will respect or disrespect for the former pastor influence the attitude of members toward any man he suggests to the committee?[4] Neighboring or even distant pastors who are held in esteem by the church may be contacted, and often provide helpful suggestions. Denominational leaders, friends and church members, schools, and ministers form the most fruitful sources for locating available candidates.

Unsolicited suggestions should be evaluated very carefully. More will be said about evaluating recommendations and information later in this chapter, but in answering the question, What is the best source? a committee might consider two comments by experienced pulpit committeemen: (1) "The best source to turn to for prospective pastor suggestions is one that knows your church well, knows the men he suggests as well, and has contact with a fairly large number of preachers"; (2) "I would first ask the advice of a man whose judgment I had confidence in, one who I thought would be more interested in the welfare of my church than in just finding a position for a preacher."[5]

Once a list of possible candidates is secured, the wise pulpit committee will not immediately go off on a "shopping trip" for the best bargain—hearing this man and that man to make comparisons. Much time and travel expense can be saved by first exploring sources of information about the men under consideration.

DETERMINE SOURCES OF INFORMATION ABOUT CANDIDATES

Not only does the committee concern itself about sources of possible names of candidates, but also about sources for information about the possible candidates. Although some churches are fearful to ask anything about anyone because they feel this is below the dignity of the church, and especially that of the clergy, a few churches have gone to the other extreme of hiring a private investigator. A balance must be followed. There is no excuse, with our modern means of communication, for a church not to obtain all the information necessary concerning a prospective candidate. Instant information is available at relatively low-cost telephone rates. A few cents speeds a letter to any place in the United States within hours.

Denominational officers and records. Most denominations, either on a district or national level, or both, keep current biographical information on all pastors in its ministerial association. Much of this information is available upon request. Often personal interviews with district superintendents or home missions secretaries provide valuable guidance to the pulpit committee. There is no reason to distrust these men. The denomination is only as strong as its local churches. For this, if for no other reason, denominational leaders desire to see the local church strong and productive under adequate leadership. The denominational leader who is usually closest to a pastor is his district superintendent or association secretary. The general patterns of a pastor's ministry are observed by such leaders; and the needs of the local church without a pastor are also well understood by the same leader. These men can be invaluable in assisting the church to find the most adequate man to fill its pastoral needs.

Denominational yearbooks. The denominational yearbook will usually give financial and membership reports that give some indication of the pastor's present ministry. Although the amount of information varies with the denominations, this source should not be overlooked.

Pastors. Inquiry ought to be made among other pastors; especially those who are well acquainted with the prospective candidate. Many times these men are able to give peculiar insight into the character of the man and his work. This kind of inquiry does not have to be extensive. Contact with a few carefully chosen and representative men will provide the information the committee seeks. If the prospect is not immediately serving a church, the pastor of the church of which he is a member should be contacted. Other clergymen who have served on committees or in united efforts with the minister under consideration may also give helpful information. A note to the district or national headquarters will bring information about what committees or boards he has served on, along with the names of those with whom he has served.

School records. Grades and accomplishments academically should be checked. Instructors can give further information. School records and interviews with school officials can give an indication as to the man's dedication, diligence, ability, leadership, burden for people and personal idiosyncracies.

Other records. Some churches may feel embarrassed to ask for a credit rating on a prospective pastor, yet such a procedure could prove very enlightening in certain situations. Such an investigation should always be done discreetly. If the minister has served in the military, a request for a recommendation from one or two of his commanding officers could be helpful.

The study of records is important, but should never be the sole criterion. Records can give a false picture because much of the preacher's work is not tabulated except by God in His own record book.

Candidate's past and present pastorates. Someone who has had the minister as his pastor would be a good source of information. The attempt here should be for a balanced viewpoint by checking with a number of people. Do not emphasize negatives, but attempt to obtain information about the man's strong points. His administrative ability and programming adaptability can be evaluated best by other church staff members who have served with him. If a visit to his present or former church's community is possible, what people in that community have to say about the man will be helpful, especially in regard to his impact, influence, and acceptability in the community. Ideally, the rapport between the church seeking a pastor and the church whose pastor they are considering should be on such a level that a confidential evaluation of the man and his ministry can be obtained.

The minister himself. Preliminary investigations for information may be accomplished by an initial letter to determine whether the prospect has any interest in considering the possibility of candidating. Some churches use a questionnaire that is mailed to prospective candidates. This questionnaire may accompany the initial inquiry, but not until he has consented to be considered as a candidate should he be expected to complete it. (See Appendix E for a prospective candidate questionnaire and accompanying letter used by the Immanuel Baptist Church of Waukegan, Illinois.) Such a questionnaire may become the basis for further investigation, or it may be sufficient in itself to indicate that no further contact should be made. If so, the minister should be notified immediately. Other churches use a more formal candidating application form. This has merit, but should be used only as a second step, never as part of the initial inquiry. This form could request names of persons to contact as references. (See Appendix F.) Certain groups also use questionnaire forms that are sent to references for completion. (See Appendix D).

The investigation should include hearing the prospective pastor in his own pulpit by the committee or its representatives. In this way the pastor is seen and heard in familiar surroundings, with the organist and choir director he is used to. He will exhibit his usual behavior, and his normal sermon delivery will be appreciated. All things being equal, this encounter should always precede any invitation to preach in the pulpit of the church which seeks a pastor. Some valuable information can be gained by arranging for an appointment with the pastor in his study during the afternoon of the visit, or possibly some weekday. This should not be a surprise visit, but planned and asked for in advance.

Almost immediately the committee members can get an idea of the man's industry, interests, and love for people. A glance at his library and a survey of his staff provide further helpful insight. If interest on the pastor's part is definite, the committee may discuss the pastor's job specifications, or at least outline what their church expects of its pastor. Some description of the church, pastor's study, and parsonage may be given. All other things being satisfactory, the committee may ask if the minister would be willing to consider being a candidate. Some time should be spent by the committee members in talking with church members and others in the community concerning the man. If the committee decides not to consider him further, they should notify him immediately.

Having close contact with the man over an extended period of time is ideal. It is the best way to get to know him. This, however, is usually not possible. Occasionally a church finds itself in the position of considering a man who has been a member of the church, has lived or served nearby, or has ministered in the church on numerous occasions for special meetings or conferences. This situation certainly makes the candidating procedure less complicated. Foote suggests a plan that is by nature practical only in the case of an unattached candidate.

> Ask him to come as a supply for one, two or three months, [so] that the church may make acquaintance, with the understanding that at the end of the stated period the connection may be made a permanent one if mutually agreeable, either party, however, being at liberty to withdraw if a definite settlement seems undesirable. Where this method is followed the church should pay the candidate's traveling expenses and his usual salary during the stipulated period.[6]

Not all the sources listed above will be used in every case, and the order in which the sources are mentioned does not necessarily have to be followed, although it does constitute a suggested chronology. In any case, contact with the man himself should not be first, and usually should be last.

After considering the best possible sources for information, the pulpit committee must eventually decide what information they want to obtain. (This will be considered later in this chapter.)

USE OF INFORMATION SOURCES

The "how to" of using these sources should be the next concern of the pulpit committee in its procedural outline. Phone calls are certainly the most timesaving way, but often do not provide the detail of information necessary. However, phone calls are cheaper than long automobile or plane rides and can provide much preliminary information. Some recommend the use of the phone because they feel certain persons more freely express themselves verbally than in writing. It is, however, always best to obtain written information and recommendations. This protects the confidant from being misunderstood or misquoted. Letters are inexpensive and quickly put one in touch with any part of the country. (Since most mail travels by air these days anyway, reserve your airmail stamps for foreign letters. If you feel that an airmail stamp would speed up delivery, check with your post office.) Sometimes a church has difficulty in obtaining addresses for writing inquiry letters. The denominational yearbook is the answer here, as well as district or association records. These are always available from denominational headquarters and district workers.

COURTESY TOWARD OTHER CHURCHES

One further policy the pulpit committee should place in its procedural outline is that of its relationship with and courtesy toward the sister church whose pastor is being seriously considered as a possible candidate. This area is often unintentionally overlooked simply because a church gets so involved with its own needs and desires. The committee may well ask itself: Has due consideration been given in the proposed call of the pastor, to the interests and welfare of the church from which he is being called or considered? Should a church ruthlessly and inconsiderately seek to take away the pastor of a sister church? Bailey puts it this way: "Has a church a right to disturb a man who is doing an oustanding work for the Lord, and who is happily at work in his section of the great Vineyard?"[7]

These are serious questions and must be considered by any well-meaning church. It may be true that no church possesses any exclusive right to any minister, but there are some built-in courtesies that should be observed on the basis of mutual Christian love. On the other hand, every minister should be in the place where his services can be most effective. A vacant church should act on this principle in calling to its service the pastor of another church. But it should act kindly with concern toward the other church. The church whose pastor is under study or call by another church must also presume that this motive of suiting the minister to his most effective place of service is directing the inquiry.

REDUCING THE POTENTIAL LIST OF CANDIDATES

As stated above, another concern of the pulpit committee is the need to reduce the list of possible candidates to a workable number of about four or five—those who appear most likely to meet the qualifications based on the needs of the church. A simple typed letter of inquiry assists in this job. (See Appendix E.) *Never use a form letter.*

> It is a good procedure at this point to determine either by letter or by telephone whether the candidate might be willing to consider a call to your church in the event it were to be extended. In this way a good deal of travel, time, and money will be saved. To insure that the prospective candidate has sufficient information about your church to indi-

cate tentative interest, it is wise to supply, along with your letter, a copy of your self-study of the church or a similar form. Be sure that all envelopes addressed to prospective candidates are always marked "personal" and "confidential" and that the minister is free to speak on a confidential matter when you telephone him at this or any other time during the process.[8]

There should be no mass mailing of such a letter. Only the four or five most eligible should receive it. This initial list of candidates can be arrived at through prayerful review of each person under consideration in light of his background and recommendations received. If each committee member will then rank the top three against the qualifications desired based on the needs of the church, tabulation will provide this initial list of four or five potential candidates.

GATHERING INFORMATION

When a minister indicates his willingness to be considered as a candidate, serious investigation of the man is the next step for the pulpit committee. So important is this procedure that a whole section of this chapter is given to it (see pp. 82-88).

VISITING THE CANDIDATE

When a pulpit committee visits a church after thorough investigation of the man in light of its own church's needs, then goes in a spirit of love and concern for the church visited, they need not feel guilty or apologetic. Members of both churches should view such procedures with mutual dependence upon God for His will to be done. His will is always best for all concerned. He does not shortchange one church to benefit another. The pulpit committee should bathe the visit in much prayer, seeking to enter into the spirit of the service and not just observe as critics. Nevertheless, committee members should be observant. They should be aware of the general atmosphere. Is there reverence and orderliness? What of the music? How do the people participate and respond? How well does the minister communicate? Is his delivery good? Has he developed a friendly church?

This visit in the prospective candidate's church should be built on a solid preliminary study of the man and his work. It should be only one factor among many by which a decision is made. An interview with the man, preferably after the visit, should be arranged, as an informal, unhurried session.

THE CANDIDATE'S VISIT

If after careful inquiry, investigation, and evaluation of information obtained, and after a visit to his present church, a minister is requested to candidate and agrees to visit the church, the pulpit committee should have determined in some detail the procedure to be followed during the visit. As for the length of the visit, a long weekend is better than one Sunday; and a full week including two Sundays is ideal. This will allow him to spend the intervening week with the people and to learn something of the character of the community and church. It may be in order for the prospective candidate to urge, or to at least state his willingness to wait until a week with two Sundays is available. Too often candidating takes place during the summer months to coincide with a minister's vacation. July and August are probably the worst months to candidate because so many people are on vacation; thus the congregation is not representative. What the visit should include, and courtesies due the candidate, will be considered later.

THE CONTRACTUAL AGREEMENT

Another concern of the pulpit committee in the procedural outline is how the candidate will be presented to the church body for vote, if the committee so decides. The local church's constitution should provide guidelines for this. Some churches feel that any preliminary mention of salary is akin to being unspiritual, so they often leave it as a last consideration. For example, one pastor said, "In churches I have pastored they have requested me to visit for a Sunday and preach. They usually have a congregational meeting next and vote to see how many, or if all, agree to give me a call. Then I meet with the board to see if I agree with their terms and salary." This personal encounter over finances may cause unnecessary embarrassment and possible ill feelings which provide poor basis to inaugurate a church-pastor relationship. If financial arrangements are not determined beforehand, it would be more advisable to include them in the letter of call.

The vote to call the candidate should be considered by itself. Other decisions such as salary should be voted on separately. The church should appreciate that it is entering into a contract with the candidate; if he accepts, the church itself has certain responsibilities already agreed to by its vote. In some churches the pastor's salary and other benefits are currently fixed and thus can be discussed with the candidate prior to his visit, or even placed in the initial letter of contact (see Appendix E). This procedure is preferred.

THE LETTER OF CALL

If the vote is positive, the pulpit committee then has the privilege of writing the letter of call. This must be very delineative with no possibility of misunderstanding. Nothing should be presumed or assumed.

PROCEDURAL INVESTIGATION AND PLANNING BY
THE PULPIT COMMITTEE

On the part of both the church and the pastor there is good evidence that too often the difficulty of investigation has obscured necessary frankness. Many men have been broken and many churches severed on the rack of an embarrassed and artificial naiveté. Erdman has well said, "The fuller the knowledge possessed by both parties, the larger the promise of satisfaction and success."[9]

PROCEDURAL CHECK LIST

From our present study it may be possible to outline a procedural checklist for the pulpit committee. Not all churches will see fit to follow every section of the outline, but it will help the committee to be more thorough.

1. Is prayer for guidance being sincerely offered?
2. Is the church ready and willing to be led of the Holy Spirit in its choice?
3. Has prayerful selection been made of an adequate, representative, and dependable pulpit committee?
4. Has a brief but honest self-study been made to determine needs and related pastoral qualifications?
5. Has an adequate pastoral job specification been drawn up?
6. Has sufficient and up-to-date information been gathered concerning the church so that intelligent answers can be given to the candidate's questions?
7. Has it been agreed that the needs of the candidate and his family will also be carefully investigated and evaluated in the total picture?
8. Has the committee determined to first consider the qualifications of the men best suited to the needs of the church?
9. Has the committee agreed to present to the church only one man at a time?
10. Has it been agreed that careful and thorough investigation and inquiry will be the essential policy?
11. Has the committee agreed to narrow the list of possibilities to a few worthy and desirable men to thoroughly investigate?
12. Is it understood that this investigation will be done before the man is invited to visit the church?
13. Have the possible sources for names and information been determined and agreed upon?
    a. Denomination sources

    b. Friends and members of the church

    c. Fellow pastors

    d. School and other records

    e. Present and past pastorates of candidate

    f. Candidate himself

14. Have visits been made to hear the man preach in his own pulpit and to view the work of his present pastorate?

15. Has a tentative outline been made as to the procedure of the candidate's visit to the church so that the visit will be meaningful and efficient?

16. Has the procedure of submitting a candidate to the church along with his qualifications been outlined so that sufficient information is given for an intelligent vote by the people?

17. Have the contents of the call letter been tabulated and outlined so that sufficient information will be given the candidate for his serious consideration?

We will expand on some of these points in the following pages, but our immediate concern in this chapter is how to use these sources. What important information should the church obtain concerning the minister being considered for the pastoral position? The following lists give suggestions for the pulpit committee to consider in an investigation of a potential candidate.

All areas are related to the spiritual life of the individual. Therefore, a specific section about the pastor's spiritual life is not listed per se. Spiritual qualifications are best determined indirectly through careful observation in the entire candidating procedure. The overall question should be, Does he conform to the scriptural qualifications of 1 Timothy 3 and Titus 1?

Another most important consideration that will affect many other areas of a man's ministry is his philosophy of the purpose and ministry of the local church. This should be thoroughly sounded out to make sure his philosophy is the same as the church considering him.

PRELIMINARY INVESTIGATION

Although most of the following considerations can be determined before an actual interview with the candidate, there are some, especially those with an asterisk, that will be answered more thoroughly through a personal interview or by hearing the man preach.. When the questions can be considered both before and during the personal encounter, more complete will be the answers. The church entering such careful investigation of a potential pastor must do so with full appreciation that no man is perfect. No minister can be found acceptable in all of the areas listed below. *The lists are given merely as guidelines. It is not the author's intention that they be used in entirety for each investigation.* Remember, no church will find a perfect pastor, but they can find the right one.

THE CANDIDATE'S PERSONAL LIFE

  1. What kind of husband and father is he? Is he able to manage his own household?
 * 2. What is his attitude toward the privacy of his home?
 * 3. What is his wife like? Is she an asset or a liability to him? How does he consider the role of his wife in the work of the church?
 * 4. Are his children well behaved? Are they Christians?
  5. Does he control his temper?
  6. How old is he?
  7. What are his personal habits in regard to cleanliness and hygiene?§
  8. Is he lazy or industrious?
 * 9. Is he neat and conservative in dress and personal appearance?
 * 10. Is he orderly of mind in his personal affairs?
 * 11. How well does he handle money? What is his attitude

§A pastor's wife once indicated that about all she could remember of one pastor she and other girls worked for in vacation Bible school one summer was the "green moss" on his teeth.

toward money? Does he pay his debts? Does he live on credit?‖ What does he consider an adequate salary?

* 12. How is his health?

* 13. Does he have good study habits?

14. Is he emotionally healthy and psychologically secure?

15. Is he a man of integrity?

16. What is his moral record?

17. What kind of a personal devotional life does he have?

THE CANDIDATE'S PERSONALITY

* 1. Is he a courteous and kindly man with a genius for friendship?

* 2. Does he have some power of drawing to himself the old and the young, the known and the stranger?

* 3. Is he easy to become acquainted with or is he somewhat distant?

* 4. Does he have qualities which inspire respect, confidence, and affection?

5. Is he fair-minded, well poised, and tactful?

6. Is he skillful in avoiding quarrels, yet courageous and firm in standing by basic Christian convictions?

7. Can he be fair to those who disagree with him?

8. Is he able to speak and act with sound judgment and mature thought even under emotional strain?

9. Is he flexible? Is he able to grow and change?

10. What do members of his present church and former churches think of him? (This question should also be asked under "The Candidate's Ability as Pastor and Preacher.")

11. What do his neighbors and people in his community think of him? (This question should also be asked in

‖"One thing that cannot be tolerated in any minister of Christ is financial looseness or irregularity. The minister who is always in debt, and who leaves a legacy of unpaid claims behind him in every parish is never able, by the eloquence of the pulpit, to counteract the damage done by his example" (Washington Gladden, *The Christian Pastor and the Working Church* [New York: Scribner, 1911], p. 82).

relationship to "The Candidate's Ability as Pastor and Preacher.")

12. What do those on his present and former church staffs think of him? (This should also be asked in relationship to "The Candidate's Ability as Pastor and Preacher.")

13. How do other pastors and denominational workers regard him personally?

14. How does he get along with other people?

15. What types of people does he work with best?

16. Has he had many personality clashes?

* 17. Does he possess some good knowledge of human nature, and something of that saving sense of humor which serves as a lubricant of life's frictions?

18. Will he command the respect of the people of the community?

19. How will the leaders of the community regard him?

20. Can he relate to the culturally deprived with genuine concern for them?

21. What is his attitude toward people of other races and social strata?

THE CANDIDATE'S DOCTRINAL BELIEFS

* 1. Does he agree with the doctrinal statement of the church?

2. Does he have any doctrinal idiosyncracies that he "rides as a hobby?"

3. Are there any indications of unorthodox or peculiar doctrinal stands?

* 4. What is his belief concerning tithing and stewardship? How does he relate this to his teaching ministry?

* 5. What is his conviction concerning marriage of divorced people, mixed marriages, and marriage of nonbelievers?

6. What is his attitude toward church finances, suppers, sales, pledges, faith promises, etc.?

* 7. What is his attitude toward missions and stewardship?

  * 8. What is his position regarding baptism, the Lord's Supper, and dedication of infants?

  * 9. What is his concept of the separated life?

*10. What position does he take on the inspiration of Scripture?

*11. What position does he take on the new morality and situation ethics?

*12. Do his doctrinal beliefs have a positive effect on his own life?

  13. How does he think the Bible relates to an active ministry by the church in social problems?

THE CANDIDATE'S BACKGROUND AND TRAINING

1. What early home boyhood influences still manifest themselves?

* 2. When was he converted? Under what circumstances? What did the experience mean to him?

3. Does he have any particular handicaps?

4. What information is available concerning his parents, brothers and sisters that could reflect upon his ministry?

5. Where did he take his college work?

6. Of what theological seminary is he a graduate? Does this school hold to any specific, peculiar, or questionable doctrine?

7. What do his transcripts from these schools indicate about his dependability, industry, etc.?

8. What degrees has he earned? Are they really an index to his scholarly habits and ability?

9. What leadership ability did he evidence, and what class offices did he hold during his schooling?

THE CANDIDATE'S PROFESSIONAL CAREER AND EXPERIENCE

1. What positions has he held? With what success?

* 2. Why did he leave his last position or why does he want to leave it?

3. Has he been accepted/popular in the community? With whom and by reason of what qualities?

4. What does the program, status, and growth of his present church indicate? This should include all areas such as worship services, Sunday school, youth programs, missionary program, social action, etc.

5. Is he a proven administrator?

6. What is his attitude toward his staff and fellow workers at his present or former churches?

7. What is the indebtedness, financial status, and program of his present church?

8. Where has he excelled and what are his special interests? What weaknesses are indicated?

9. Is he a builder who leaves a church stronger than he found it?

10. How does he stand with men, with women, with youth, with children, with the outside community?

11. What frustration has he experienced or is he experiencing in the ministry?

*12. Were the churches he has served large or small, new or old, city or country, growing or declining? Was his ministry effective in light of the opportunities and circumstances?

*13. What community leadership positions has he held? With what success?

*14. What positions has he held on the district or national level with the denomination? With what contribution?

15. How do other pastors and denominational workers regard his work?

16. What does his record indicate as to his cooperation with other churches, denominational programs, community, and social projects?

17. Does he have a good grasp of contemporary life, or is he somewhat removed from reality?

THE CANDIDATE'S ABILITY AS A PASTOR

1. How concerned is he with helping others?
2. What place in his ministry does he give to personal counseling?
3. What type of counseling is he adept at? Counseling youth? Comforting the sorrowing? Hospital visitation?
4. What success has he had in premarital and marital counseling?
5. What ability does he have as a soul winner?
6. Has he a heart for people—to weep with those who weep and rejoice with those who rejoice?
7. What does his record indicate about his ministry of home visitation?
8. Does he have leadership ability and has this been evident in his pastorates?
9. Can he organize and inspire his associates in the work of the church?
10. Will his counsel and judgment be sought and increasingly respected the longer he lives in town?
11. Above all, is he a man of God, with deep and genuine convictions?
*12. Is he capable of making the church a sanctuary and its worship an experience of spiritual reality?
13. Does he have a grasp of youth and their ways of thinking?
14. Is he able to motivate a church into a united, working body, or does he have a tendency to do it all himself?
15. Does he see the church in its relation to community and world politics?
16. Does he have a heart for the world as well as for his church and community?
17. Is there evidence of creativity—an ability to find new approaches to old problems?
18. Does he finish a program once it is started?
19. What is his policy concerning church finances, budget, etc.?

20. What is the spiritual level of his present church as a result of his ministry?

THE CANDIDATE'S ABILITY AS A PREACHER

1. Is there a sense of spiritual thoroughness to his preaching? Is it Bible centered?
2. Is there more than elegance of manner or elocutionary brillance? Is there depth to his sermons?
* 3. Is his preaching powerful in conveying spiritual truths to hearts and minds?
* 4. What ability does he have as a teacher?
5. Where is his strength in the pulpit? As an evangelist, recruiter, teacher?
* 6. Is there breadth to his preaching? Does he reach the young as well as the old?
7. Is the scriptural basis of his preaching broad in its scope, or is it nearly all in one area or division?
8. Do his sermons inform, teach, uplift, challenge?
9. Are his sermons clear? Easily followed by the young?
*10. Does he have any unpleasant or repulsive mannerisms?
*11. Besides preaching, can he lead people into genuine worship?
12. What attitude does he have toward music in the church?
13. In his preaching expository, textual, topical, or a mixture?
14. Does he concentrate on social problems per se, or does he relate these to his expository preaching in a vital approach?
15. Does he honestly deal with current social concerns from a biblical viewpoint?

DATA TO BE GAINED FROM INTERVIEW

The following considerations can usually be determined through a personal interview or hearing the candidate preach. In regard to questions about the doctrinal beliefs of the candidate, it may be advisable in some instances to have a Bible college or seminary graduate as an appointed member of the committee for that part of the interview. In theology the meaning of words change and this problem of semantics may be overcome by the assistance of such a person. If one such person is a member of the church, it may wisely appoint him as a regular member of the pulpit committee.

HIS PERSONAL LIFE

Much can be learned concerning the minister's personal and home life through observation.

HIS PERSONALITY

Careful observation of his emotional stability is essential. His ease and security in talking about himself, his strengths and weaknesses should be evaluated.

HIS DOCTRINAL BELIEFS

How would the candidate summarize his doctrinal position? A request to read his statements given at the time of his ordination may be in order here. The committee should ask, however, if he has changed any of his convictions since that time.

HIS STUDY HABITS

1. What is his attitude toward the formal training he has had?
2. Does he desire more schooling?
3. What are his present reading habits? How many books a year does he read? What magazines and periodicals does he subscribe to?
4. What hours does the candidate desire to spend in study without interruption, except for emergencies?

HIS PROFESSIONAL CAREER AND EXPERIENCE

1. What type of ministry does he prefer or feel most adequate in? Which is he most efficient and productive in?
2. Does he demonstrate the use of God-given gifts?

HIS ABILITY AS A PASTOR

1. What title does he prefer: Reverend, Minister, Pastor, or first name?
2. How does he handle premarital and marital counseling?
3. How does he handle particular problems in the church? (The committee may pose a true-to-life situation and ask how he would deal with it.)
4. How does he plan to involve the deacons in the ministry of the church?
5. Does he have a policy of informing and/or asking the governing board permission to accept outside speaking engagements?
6. Does he usually inform the deacons when he must be away for over twenty-four hours?
7. Why is he in the ministry?

HIS ABILITY AS A PREACHER

1. What does he believe to be biblical preaching?
2. What is his objective or goal in preaching?
3. Why does he want to preach?

Special attention should be given to the physical health of the prospective candidate. Too often this is overlooked, with occasional upsetting results. There is no reason why a church should not require the serious potential candidate to have a physical examination with the report sent to the pulpit committee by the physician. The inquiring church should pay for the examination. What great value this would be to the minister and the church if some hidden physical ailment were uncovered in time and readily treated! The cost for such a physical examination is small compared to the benefit gained. The church is put at ease concerning the minister's health, and a real need is met in the pastor's life. Frequently a pastor's salary causes him to put off such important things.

In conclusion, two cautions must be noted. No church should consider or admit to its pulpit, not even for a single service, a man who does not come with the clearest, amplest, and most recent credentials of ministerial standing. Secondly, a message from the pulpit is meaningless and can be detrimental, no matter how eloquent or stirring it is, unless it is backed by a life. The preacher must practice what he preaches.

USING AND TESTING RECOMMENDATIONS

The experience of many pulpit committees indicates quite clearly that not every source of information has the same value and that not every recommendation can be taken at face value. Leonard Hill provides some quotations from frustrated pulpit committees which show quite clearly that this is often the case.

> When we first got the letter of recommendation, we thought we'd found the ideal pastor. But then we discovered the man recommending him was his brother-in-law.

> Our committee got twenty-five letters of recommendation for the same man. But when every letter sounded almost the same, we wouldn't have called him to be our janitor.

> What is a church going to do when you can't even trust preachers? Two pastors recommended a man to our church who had been fired from his last two pastorates for immoral conduct.

> It was a glowing letter of recommendation. But it should have been. The man wrote it himself.[10]

What complicates the problem is that in the United States not a few ministerial vagrants are still active. Many of them are plausible villains, with smooth tongues and taking ways, who are able to do incalculable injury to those churches which harbor them even for a day. There are also men who have failed because of their own lack of dedication to Christ and are not willing to repent and make things right. Thus they are frustrated to the point of trying to get a church even by dishonest means, simply to make a living.

OFFICIAL RECOMMENDATIONS

Official recommendations from denominational officers or leaders are usually the most trustworthy and factual. It is true that some denominational workers and even pastors refuse to recommend a man to a church, but simply give all the information available and leave the matter entirely up to the church. This is hardly a satisfactory method and innately engenders suspicion.

SAFETY IN NUMBERS

There is safety in numbers. More than one recommendation is essential. One glowing recommendation may be offset by another negative one, but this is far better than acting on a single glowing recommendation with ignorance of the possible negative statements. A good rule to follow is that for every good recommendation seek out another one to balance or substantiate it.

To say the least, the task of evaluating recommendations is not easy, but when a number of independent recommendations are positive, and the results of other investigations agree, that man may be seriously considered.

WHAT A RECOMMENDATION SHOULD CONTAIN

Because many people do not know how to write recommendations, the pulpit committee may find it advantageous to outline the content of a letter of recommendation or request return of a questionnaire giving ample room for personal comments. (See Appendix D). A recommendation should contain at least three parts: (1) Information about the person; (2) evaluation of the minister's abilities in light of the needs of the church; and (3) commendation to the church if such is warranted.[11] If such an outline is followed, it will prevent the recommender from simply commending the man. A meaningful recommendation must explain *why* the minister is recommended. A person may write and make some general statement that he knows the church well and the prospective candidate well, and that he thus would heartily recommend him as the pastor. This is somewhat helpful but not detailed enough for the pulpit committee to use as a very valuable tool in its inquiry. A letter of recommendation which says, "I'm sorry that I do not know the person very well, and all I have heard is good, and he appears to be a man of fine Christian character, therefore I feel he would make you a good pastor, and he has my recommendation," has very little value to the pulpit committee.

Some pulpit committees tend to disregard a recommendation that does not indicate that the person making the recommendation feels that the Holy Spirit is leading him to so recommend the man. This is a dangerous tendency because God's will for a particular church usually is not indicated vicariously. In fact, such statements may tend to cloud the matter. Too many times the Holy Spirit gets blamed or credited for some very important decisions that He had no part in at all. The Holy Spirit leads practically, orderly, and decently, and usually on the basis of factual information. Unless the recommender feels very strongly about including a comment about the Holy Spirit's leading, it would be best to omit such a statement and allow the Holy Spirit to use the information given along with other accumulated facts. The vast majority of recommendations do not presume to know how God will lead in the matter. This is always best. The recommender should take the passive role of attempting to inform the pulpit committee about the minister and why he may be a good person for the committee to seriously consider.

MAKING THE BEST USE OF RECOMMENDATIONS AND
INFORMATION

Another concern in this category is knowing how to make best use of a recommendation when it is received. The pulpit committee may spend some very valuable time in studying the characteristics of a good recommendation and thus be able to make more intelligent and meaningful use of it when it arrives. It is easy to identify a letter that has as its main objective the welfare of the minister, with little concern for the church. Such a letter is of limited value. A good recommendation will indicate a definite interest in the welfare of the church seeking a pastor. Again let it be said that a letter that presumes to embody the will of God for the church has questionable overtones. The following suggestions may be of value to the pulpit committee in evaluating letters of recommendation.[12]

1. *The source must be trustworthy and knowledgeable.* The committee will save itself much anxiety if it is careful to request recommendations from persons whose integrity and judgment they can trust because of personal and close acquaintance or because of position in the denomination. A person of high respect and integrity and fully acquainted with the one he recommends, but one who does not know the church requesting the recommendation, cannot provide as adequate a recommendation as one who knows both the man and the church well. The committee will do well to keep the recommendations cataloged into three areas: (a) knows minister well; (b) knows church well; (c) knows both the minister and church well.

2. *The extent of knowledge must be adequate.* A good recommendation will reveal how well the person making the recommendation knows the prospective pastor and his work. It will also indicate how long he has known him. An acceptable recommendation will also give opportunity to state how much the recommender knows about the ministry (needs and opportunities) of the church requesting the recommendation.

3. *The scope of information must be inclusive.* The helpful recommendation will provide both negative and positive statements. No person is perfect. Specific and general comments concerning strong and weak points provide the most helpful kind of information.

4. *The commendation must be reasonable.* A recommendation without an explanation of why, fails to be adequate. Although the recommender may have limited knowledge, he should be requested to state why he recommends or does not recommend the man. The purpose of recommendations is to find a man suited to the particular church involved.

5. *The information must have pertinence.* Many glowing adjectives, but with little meaty relevance, provide a recommendation of questionable value.

6. *The letter of recommendation must not be presumptuous.* A recommendation that attempts to place the Holy Spirit's stamp of approval on the minister as the man for the church has built-in suspicion. If such is stated upon definite conviction, it must be accompanied by a recommendation that measures up to the above five points. The Holy Spirit usually leads in a practical and informative way.

Don't expect a perfect recommendation. Such will probably never be written. Nevertheless, each recommendation should be carefully examined for the above factors. This will enable the pulpit committee to determine recommendations of greatest value.

Lloyd M. Perry of Trinity Evangelical Divinity School suggests four marks of authority. These may provide some assistance to a pulpit committee in evaluating recommendations or choosing persons for recommendation. The four ways to judge authority are:

1. Does the person have official signs of respectability?
2. Is the person in agreement with other authorities of equal stature?
3. Is the person in a position really to know?
4. Is the person's authority credible?

Recommendations complement each other. Therefore it is

important to obtain recommendations from a number of different sources. All recommendations should be in writing so they can be filed and compared with others. Written recommendations also require a little more thought than off-the-cuff remarks, and therefore are more valuable. Every request for a recommendation must be accompanied by the statement that all information will be kept in strict confidence as far as relating the information to its source in any way whatever. The committee must guard itself in this trust very carefully. If some particular information becomes very important to the church, it must never be released to the church without written consent of the person who provided the information. Some pulpit committees agree to destroy all letters of recommendation after a pastor has been secured. This is a good practice.

THE ACTUAL CANDIDATING ENCOUNTER

PREPARATORY CONSIDERATIONS

The encounter of candidate with church and church with candidate should have a preliminary step. If, after careful investigation of information and recommendations, a pulpit committee finds a minister that commands their special attention, a plan of encounter should be established. This first step may be a personal interview with the pastor in his study or at a neutral meeting place, such as a restaurant. Much can be learned from this interaction as outlined previously. Sometimes this interview is combined with a small representation of the pulpit committee visiting the prospect's church to hear him preach. If there has been a cordial exchange between his church and theirs concerning the committee's interests, there is no reason why an interview with the pastor cannot be requested that afternoon in his study. This is especially germane if the representatives have traveled some distance. It may also be helpful to make a brief visit to the minister's home. At any rate, it is usually best to have at least one interview with the man and hear him at least once in his own pulpit before he is considered to preach in the church seeking a pastor. To incur the inconvenience of the minister, the upset to his church, and a pseudo hope to the committee's church by inviting him to preach before every preliminary investigation is completed, is presumptuous and awkward.

The actual candidating encounter in the vacant pulpit should be the final step. It should never be considered except for a man who has the basic qualifications and who has indicated a possibility of his moving to a different pastorate. It is not out of order to ask the man during a preliminary interview if he would consider leaving his present work for a church similar to the one outlined by the pulpit committee. No question that seeks a specific answer concerning his interest in the church should be asked, but simply a request for his willingness to consider the possibility. If after this preliminary interview the committee decides not to consider the man further, *he should be so notified immediately!*

In every aspect of the actual encounter there are certain courtesies due the minister. Frankness and fairness must be the guiding principles. Pastors often complain that some pulpit committees fail to reveal significant facts about their churches. It is often too easy to require full information from the candidate, but to be apprehensive about exposing certain aspects of the church's ministry and life. One church sends a notebook to the candidate with pictures of the work, statistics on the community, constitution of the church and manual of operation. This practice provides the minister with many helpful facts and establishes a good basis for meaningful discussion when he visits the church.# When both the pulpit committee and the candidate have agreed to submit in advance a list of questions or requests for information, then the actual meeting will be more productive and will lessen the possibility for embarrassment. If denominations and/or districts would provide guidelines for such questions there would

#For a consideration of what the candidate should know about the church considering him, see Gerald W. Gillaspie, *The Restless Pastor* (Chicago: Moody, 1974).

be less reticence to follow this procedure. No party would feel embarrassed or feel that a certain line of questioning is out of order. Hiding church problems will not help get the right man as pastor. Revealing them may help the candidate to conclude that he is not adequate to handle the problems; or the right man may be challenged by them. He will certainly respect the frankness and confidence of the church in sharing the complete information—good and bad—with him. A preacher who is really interested in the possibility of pastoring a church that has made overtures will obtain the information he feels he needs in order to make an intelligent decision. If he learns of information from other sources that should have been furnished by the pulpit committee, he will have less confidence in the church than if they had been fully open and honest with him from the start.

The church must be very frank concerning its doctrinal statement and particular or peculiar beliefs. The pastor should receive a doctrinal statement before he arrives to candidate. Any further refinement of doctrinal position should be made clear during the preliminary interview; certainly no later than the candidating encounter. At the conclusion of his first service a new pastor found himself in serious trouble with many church leaders because he had led the congregation in the Lord's Prayer. The church leaders had failed to inform their pastor during the candidating procedure of the church's dispensational views which excluded the Lord's Prayer from the church services. There were still other beliefs that did not coincide with the new pastor's views. That pastorate lasted one year.

COURTESIES DUE THE MINISTER: USING THE TIME EFFECTIVELY

The candidate should fully understand that the church will cover all his expenses. If he is coming from some distance, it is best to send in advance the plane or train tickets for him and his wife. When the candidating minister arrives (or better, before he arrives) he should be handed an outlined schedule of his appointments and interviews. This will enable him to prepare and pace himself in order to be adequate in each aspect of his visit. A full week's visit, including two Sundays, will provide a more relaxed, and thus a more valuable encounter with the minister. This is quite possible if the candidate is willing to include this in his fall or winter vacation period or is able to provide this by special arrangement with his present church. If there has been the habit of absolute honesty and that "good kind of rapport" established with his church, such a request will not be out of order.

The church should always send the candidate exact information as to the location of the church and the best route to reach it. He should know the time of day he is expected to arrive and be fully informed as to where he should go upon arrival. His overnight and meal accommodations should be fully outlined for him. It is best to provide hotel or motel accommodations for the candidate. This allows him free time to visit in the community and chat with other than members of the church. Staying with one family limits his exposure and often may result in too much food and too little sleep. This does not help the minister to be at his best. Different homes may provide some meals, which gives opportunities for broader acquaintance. Most meals, especially breakfast, should be at the motel restaurant.

If he is to travel by other than his own automobile, someone should meet him at the terminal. Some arrangements for identifying each other must be made. One pastor waited in a train station for two hours while a deacon frantically tried to find him in the crowd. He was about ready to return home when the contact was made. The cost of the candidate's transportation should always be met by the church. The honorarium for his preaching assignments should be adequate. It has been suggested that for one Sunday it should be one percent of the annual salary.[13]

Many churches desire the candidate's wife to accompany him. The majority of ministers and church leaders agree to this policy. The pastorate is a team endeavor more than in most other vocations. Although the call is to the man, his partner's attitude and feelings can definitely be a positive or negative influence on his ministry. Because of this, the church has a right to meet the wife and get to know her. Her feminine insight may be very helpful to the total picture. Whether the candidate's whole family should accompany him is questionable and determined by circumstances. Usually it is not fair to the children to be put on display.

One further expense that the church should consider is that of the supply preacher for the candidate's present church. If there has been good communication with the other church, this kindness would probably be appreciated and not misunderstood, although the offer may be graciously declined.

The time during which the candidate visits the church is valuable. The pulpit committee should plan wisely how best to use it. Too often the time is limited. The agenda must include sufficient time for meetings with the pulpit committee and the official board of the church for mutual exchange of questions and answers. The candidate's returned questionnaire, a copy of the church's constitution, latest financial statement, and annual budget should be immediately available. Conferences and meetings should be set up in advance to insure that church leaders will be present. Sufficient time must be provided for interviews with members of the staff. Ample free time should be scheduled for the minister to observe the church in action. The minister's exact responsibilities in the services should be fully outlined. Nothing should be left to chance, and the candidate should be informed of all that would be expected. A trip to and through the parsonage is essential. Many churches schedule a family gathering for an evening meal, with an informal program to enable many more of the church members to become acquainted with the prospective pastor. If the minister requests something not planned by the committee, his request should be granted if at all possible.

The candidate and his wife should be directed to tour the church facilities and visit the community, with special emphasis on shopping areas, schools, and parsonage neighborhood. Some time should be allowed for the minister to look around the church and community on his own.

During the services on the Lord's Day, the church should be prepared (possibly by certain "education" via the pulpit committee) to enter into the worship and listen to the sermon for spiritual benefit, and not attempt to be overly conscious about the man "on trial." The candidate is in a difficult position, and every common courtesy and Christian consideration should be extended to him. To eliminate some of the natural undertone of questions, some churches place a biographical sketch of the pastor as an insert in the church bulletin. One church even includes a picture and brief description of his family.

At the end of the visit it is crude and unfair to demand, or even request, an answer from the candidate before he is extended a call. "Will you come if we call you?" should never be asked a prospective pastor. One candidate experienced a church voting immediately after the evening service, then its members standing around him in a circle waiting for his answer. Such a practice is uncouth and unkind. A committee may be tempted to ask, "Are you interested at all in our church?" This is a very difficult question for the minister to answer on the spot. He may feel impelled to answer "no" under the immediate stress of the visit, but then feel led by the Holy Spirit to accept the call when the church decides to ask him to serve anyway. Every effort should be made to eliminate embarrassing and difficult situations. Crudeness and the hardness of the business world have no place in this sacred situation. This, however, does not preclude the necessity of thoroughness and objectivity.

Promptness of communication is a courtesy that must always be included in the entire candidating procedure. The candidate should come with the understanding that the results of his visit will be forthcoming within the next two weeks, and preferably within ten days. The more definite the date, the better for all concerned. If a man has candidated and is seriously considering the church, but the church fails to determine a communication date, he should let common courtesy overrule any reticence and kindly request such determination. The letter informing the minister should be short but kind. Procrastination is a pet sin of too many pulpit committees. Whenever a prospective pastor has been personally contacted by a pulpit committee and thus knows he is being considered, he should be informed immediately of any definite decision. The telephone is often the best means, but the call should always be followed by a letter of confirmation. A minister should never be kept dangling after a decision has been reached.

"Plain common sense, everyday courtesy, and Christian thoughtfulness are the primary requisites to insure that a pulpit committee or church plays fair with its prospective pastor."[14]

SUMMARY

The pulpit committee must consider the possibility of obtaining an interim pastor as it identifies the needs of the church through an adequate self-study. From this study desired pastoral qualifications will come into focus and a pastoral job description can be made. Considerations will include determining sources of possible candidates and information and the intelligent use of recommendations. A procedural checklist should be worked out. Preliminary investigation will lay the groundwork for the personal interview and the carefully planned candidating visit.

6

The Call Extended to the Candidate

The advantage of outlining the work of the pulpit committee is seen in greater dimension at the point of recommending a candidate to the church for their vote. Too many pulpit committees feel that such a recommendation completes their responsibilities. There is more.

The Vote and the Call

After a minister has appeared before the church, the committee should meet and decide, on the basis of cumulative information, whether to recommend him to the church. If the committee is satisfied that the candidate's qualifications meet the needs of the church and if under the Holy Spirit's guidance there is a consensus, a recommendation should be carefully prepared. It is most important that this be a unanimous decision of the committee.

PREPARATION OF THE RECOMMENDATION

The written recommendation is first presented to the official board of the church for their careful and prayerful review. The recommendation should state clearly the facts about the minister. It should include a brief biographical sketch, relating his background, education, experience, spiritual qualities, and abilities. It should state why the committee recommends him, why they feel he can serve the church well, why they believe the Holy Spirit has so directed. If the candidate has listed some conditions under which he is willing to be called to the church, these should be written out in full and made a part of the recommendation. Further, the statement should include what the minister is expected to do in his position as pastor of the church, and what the church promises to do for the pastor. The pulpit committee may have been authorized to make some tentative agreement with the prospective pastor regarding such things as salary, housing, and retirement plan. This often is done on the basis of what the former pastor received. However, this should not be part of the recommendation. The financial arrangements should be considered only after the church has voted on the man, unless the church has already determined this and authorized the pulpit committee to communicate such information to the candidate.

NOTIFICATION OF THE CHURCH

When the official board accepts the pulpit committee's recommendation and it appears that the mind of the Holy Spirit has been discerned, the board will notify the congregation well in advance that a recommendation is prepared and will be presented at a stated time for an open discussion of the candidate in question. It should be a time when most members can be present to enable as many as possible to have a part in the discussion and decision.

RECOMMENDATION SUBMITTED TO THE CHURCH

The recommendation is submitted by the official board to the duly called business meeting of the church. Accepted parliamentary procedure should be followed with adequate time allowed for disclosure of all pertinent information. The church, satisfied with the information received and with the recommendation, will then call for a vote. Some congregations choose to determine a subsequent time for the vote, but this is not an efficient use of time and procedure.

PRAYER AND THE VOTE

The moderator of the business meeting requests time for prayer so the whole church may lift its heart to God for wisdom and guidance. He then calls for the vote. The customary method, which allows every member to express himself, is the secret ballot.

Tellers are appointed to count the ballots and to report to the congregation. The pulpit committee should be alert not only to how many are for or against the recommendation, but also to the number who do not vote. The spirit of the service and the attitude of the people are as important as the vote itself and should also be reported to the candidate.

THE SECOND BALLOT

If the vote is favorable, but not unanimous, and a second vote is taken to make it unanimous, the candidate should be informed of the first vote tally. If the effort to make it unanimous fails, the committee is again obligated to tell the candidate exactly what has happened. Most church leaders discourage the use of a second ballot as an effort to make the vote unanimous. It is more discreet to let the first ballot stand as is. Under certain circumstances, when the vote is not unanimous, the committe may feel it best to express their thinking as to whether it is wise, in the judgment of the committee, for the minister to accept the call. If the vote is unfavorable, the prospective pastor should be immediately notified that he is no longer under consideration.

SECONDARY BUT ESSENTIAL CONSIDERATION

The actual vote should be limited to the question of issuing a pastoral call and should not include other matters which might be debatable. For example, if the church has not previously determined salary and benefits, it should vote on such *after* voting on the candidate. In other words, it is best not to vote on a motion that includes two elements—to call a man and to pay him a certain salary. If this is recommended by the pulpit committee, some member of the church should request the parliamentary procedure of dividing the question. The man must be allowed to stand on his merits alone.

If the recommendation includes salary and other financial arrangements, some members may vote against the motion, not because they oppose the man but because they feel the salary is either too much or not enough. In the motion concerning finances there should be full coverage and understanding so that the call to the minister leaves no questions or uncertainty. The call should include such items as salary; date the church desires the minister to start his work; provisions for parsonage, utilities, car expenses; length of vacation, time allowed for special speaking engagements and conferences; coverage of moving expenses; telephone expenses, book expenses, retirement benefits, parsonage and office improvements prior to the pastor's arrival, convention expenses; responsibility for church staff; time allowed for secular work and/or further schooling, pulpit supply selection and remuneration when pastor is absent. Too many churches fall short in spelling out these details and are guilty of "bargain hunting," or seeing how much they can get for as little money as possible. The result is usually disastrous.

The more detailed the understanding is in these areas, the happier the new pastor-church relationship will be. The simplest procedure is to have this whole consideration decided by the church before any candidate is considered. This allows the total financial picture to be presented to the candidate during his interaction with the the church officials, if not before. Certain circumstances, however, may dictate against this procedure. The experience (or lack of it) and potential of a certain man may indicate the need for a change in the current pay scale by the church. In any case, after the candidate receives a positive vote by the church, the pulpit committee or any other church member always has the privilege of recommending a change in the agreed salary and/or other financial arrangements. If the church has authorized the pulpit committee to stipulate the financial arrangements to the candidate, no change should be made unless it is to increase material benefits. It is very important that an annual cost-of-living adjustment in salary be agreed to by the church. This should be part of the letter of call. The letter of call should also include the pastor's job specification, even if the pastor has received a copy previously. He certainly should have. At least there should be an outline of what the church expects from the pastor, especially in the areas of visitation, evangelism, preaching, worship services, denominational cooperation, funerals, weddings, missions, church business meetings.

INFORMING THE MINISTER

If the candidate fails to obtain the desired two-thirds majority vote or fails to meet certain qualifications and thus is not recommended to the church, he should be so advised in writing—with an expression of appreciation from the chairman of the pulpit committee for his willingness to be a candidate. If the vote is favorable, the pulpit committee may desire to notify the minister by phone concerning the vote and the spirit of the meeting. This should be followed by a letter of call that contains all the agreements. (See Appendix H.) The committee should not pressure the minister for an immediate answer and never request an answer at the time of the initial phone call. If a man is expected to follow God's will in the matter, he must be given time to seek and determine God's will. Because pastors have been known to hold out longer than they should in replying to a call, it is best to ask for a reply by a certain date. Enough time should be given, however, to allow the minister to submit his resignation, or at least to inform his church officers of his intention before he replies. Every member of the church should join the prospective pastor in prayer every day as they together seek God's will in the matter. Every united prayer time should make this a priority concern.

Final Responsibilities

"If the pulpit committee has investigated well, adhered to New Testament standards, presented the prospective pastor fairly to the congregation, obtained a clear understanding of the will of the members, conveyed the call and other details agreed upon to the preacher, and through it all sought the will of God, it can truly rejoice when the man says, 'I accept.' "[1]

Too many pulpit committees stop their work before it is finished. Actually, the work of the committee is not completed until the minister has been welcomed and installed as the pastor. An additional duty then will be to make a formal report to the church of the minister's answer to the call.

All confidential material should be destroyed or returned to its original source. Care should be taken that no minister previously contacted has been left wondering about that contact.

If the church usually has a formal installation service, the pulpit committee may work with the church officers in planning this event.

PARSONAGE PREPARATIONS

If it has been outlined as the committee's responsibility, or if no one else is assigned to do it and permission is granted, the committee may oversee the preparation of the parsonage, making sure that repairs are made, interior decorating and exterior painting is done, and utilities are connected. The pastor's study should also be in complete readiness. Usually the trustees of the church do this and also are responsible for the moving arrangements for the pastor, but it might be wise for the committee to double check on the delegating of such responsibilities. If a parsonage is not provided, the church should make arrangements to assist their new pastor in finding suitable housing. In some instances temporary housing may be necessary.

One or two members of the pulpit committee should be

assigned the privilege of introducing their new pastor and family to the community. This can be done by an article and photograph in the local newspaper. The denominational magazine should also be notified. Specific personal introductions should be made to certain community and school leaders and to other local pastors. A formal presentation of the new pastor to the congregation on his first Sunday may be planned. Some churches arrange a formal, but simple reception where civic and church leaders are invited.

LETTERS OF THANKS

Letters of thanks should be written to those who have provided recommendations or have helped the pulpit committee in any way. Some type of communication may be sent to the church from which the new pastor comes, assuring them of the committee's and their church's prayerful concern as they now seek a new pastor. Institutions which have provided names of candidates should be thanked and notified that the position has been filled. Letters of thanks should also be sent to all men who were nominees for the candidacy so that they know they are no longer under consideration. This is a most important courtesy that many churches overlook.

FORMAL REPORT

A summary report of the committee's work must be made and given to the church clerk for permanent filing in the church archives. All expenses and outstanding bills incurred by the committee must be paid.

The church should formally thank the pulpit committee at the conclusion of its work and dissolve the committee, if it is ad hoc. Someone should be appointed to communicate regularly with the pastor-elect so that he receives bulletins and all important information about the church during the time before his arrival.

7

Condensed Checklist for the Pulpit Committee

1. The pulpit committee should be a small, well-chosen, and representative committee. Three to five persons can function efficiently. The suggested maximum number is nine. The major ministries of the church should be represented, with those whose ages are forty-five and under more largely represented than those above that age (pp. 51-52).
2. The term of the pulpit committee should be designated. One year is suggested (pp. 52-53).
3. Members of the pulpit committee should have delegated responsibilities with all minutes of meeting, information, and correspondence recorded with strict confidence and care (p. 53).
4. The committee's responsibilities should be determined by the church, and guidelines for procedure outlined. To serve effectively and efficiently the committee must know what the church expects and how to make reports to the members (pp. 53-55; 59; 80-81).
5. The pulpit committee should be fully acquainted with the New Testament qualifications for a pastor given in 1 Timothy 3 and Titus 1 (pp. 56-57).
6. The pulpit committee should study and determine the best way to request recommendations. More than one

letter of recommendation should be obtained for each man. It may be helpful to outline the content of a letter of recommendation so that such will provide the necessary information. All recommendations should be in writing (pp. 75; 91-93; 94-96).

7. The pulpit committee should also concern itself with the proper way to evaluate recommendations. The source must be trustworthy and knowledgeable. The extent of knowledge must be adequate. The scope of information must be inclusive. The commendation must be reasonable. The information must have pertinence. The letter of recommendation must not be presumptuous (pp. 94-95).

8. The pulpit committee may desire to recommend the employment of an interim pastor. Various reasons may dictate this recommendation and the agreement with the interim pastor should be carefully stated (pp. 60-61).

9. In order to determine the qualities and abilities desired in a prospective pastor, the pulpit committee should direct a self-study of the church to determine needs and formulate a job specification for the pastor (pp. 33-34; 62-67; and Appendix A; G).

10. The pulpit committee should determine the guiding principles (1) to discover names of possible candidates; and (2) to investigate these men.
    a. One prospective pastor should be considered at a time by the church. Never should two men be voted on at the same time (pp. 57-58).
    b. All investigation and gathering of information about a man should precede the actual invitation to candidate (pp. 58-59). A checklist should be used as a guide in securing this information (pp. 82-88).

11. The pulpit committee should determine a procedural outline for the candidate's actual visit to the church (p. 78).

a. All pertinent information and statistics about the church should be gathered in a meaningful listing so intelligent communication of facts can be had with any potential pastor (pp. 63-67; Appendix C).

b. All sources of available candidates should be considered: denomination leaders, interested friends, schools, pastors (pp. 68-70).

c. All sources of information about possible candidates should be considered and utilized when deemed helpful: denominational officers, denominational yearbooks, pastors, school records and personnel, military and credit records, previous pastorates, and the candidate himself. Information received must be kept confidential (pp. 70-75).

d. Preliminary investigations for information may be accomplished by an initial letter to determine whether the prospect has any interest in being considered as a candidate. There may be some value in using a candidating application form (pp. 73-74; Appendix E; F).

e. Prayerful and careful effort must be made in reducing the potential list of candidates to a workable number of four or five (pp. 76-77).

f. Further preliminary investigation should include the minister's personal life, personality, doctrinal beliefs, background and schooling, professional career and experience, ability as a pastor and administrator, ability as a preacher. This should help narrow the immediate consideration to one person (pp. 82-88).

g. Pulpit committee members should arrange to visit the potential candidate's church and hear him in his own pulpit at least once (pp. 77-78).

h. An appointment with the interested candidate should be arranged at the time of the visit to his church or immediately thereafter. Areas that should be considered directly or indirectly are the seven points listed in point f above. Pertinent information about the minister should be obtained, and adequate information about the candidate's church should be gathered (pp. 73-74; 77-78).

i. A proper relationship with and courtesy toward any sister church whose pastor is being considered as a possible candidate must be maintained (pp. 75-76).

12. If after careful inquiry, investigation, and evaluation of information obtained, a minister is determined as a candidate, he should be invited to visit the church (p. 78).

a. Ideally, the visit should be for more than one Sunday and not during July or August. At least a long weekend should be arranged (p. 78).

b. There are certain courtesies due to the minister. Frankness and fairness must guide all procedures. All significant information about the church should be shared with the pastoral candidate. An outline of his responsibilities and appointments at the church should be given him in advance. Exact location of the church and information concerning his sleeping accommodations and meals should be forwarded to him. A check covering all expenses and an honorarium should be handed to him before he leaves (pp. 98-99).

c. The time during which the candidate is visiting the church should be used to the greatest advantage. Ample time should be given the minister to observe the church in action and to look over the community. Conferences and interviews should be arranged in advance and informal fellowship times planned (pp. 100-1).

d. A tour through the parsonage should be provided (p. 100).

e. The candidate's preaching responsibilities should be planned well in advance, and every effort should be made to eliminate any factors that could add discomfort to the minister's already difficult task (pp. 101-2).

f. No impromptu reaction should be asked of the candidate at the conclusion of the visit (p. 101).

g. The candidate should be informed as to the approximate date he will hear from the church concerning its decision (pp. 101-2).

13. The pulpit committee's responsibility includes certain facets in preparing the church to vote intelligently concerning the candidate (pp. 103-4).

a. A recommendation, in writing, is to be prepared and presented at a duly called business meeting. The recommendation should state clearly the facts about the minister and why the committee recommends him as a possible pastor of the church. If there are certain conditions under which the candidate is willing to serve, the church should be fully informed (pp. 103-4).

b. The church constituency must be notified well in advance concerning the date and time of the business meeting (p. 104).

c. At the business meeting the committee should give full information about the man and inform the church about any tentative agreements made. (Guidelines of the church's constitution should be followed.) The report should stress *why* the committee feels led by the Holy Spirit to recommend the man. Ample time and opportunity should be given for questions and comments from the people. The pulpit committee should be prepared to answer all meaningful questions fully (pp. 103-4).

d. When there are no conditions or qualifications requested by the candidate or made by the pulpit committee to the candidate, it is best to vote on the man first and then discuss and vote concerning salary, car expenses, and vacation afterwards (pp. 105-6).

e. Once the recommendation has been fully agreed upon, the chairman of the pulpit committee may desire to move that it be adopted.

f. The moderator of the business meeting will then want to call for a time of prayer, asking God to guide His people in the voting (p. 105).

g. The pulpit committee should be alert not only to how many are for or against the recommendation but also the number who do not vote and the general attitude of the people. In all fairness this also should be reported to the candidate (p. 105).

h. If the vote is favorable, the candidate may be notified (possibly by phone) of the tally of the first vote. If the vote is unfavorable, the prospective pastor should be immediately notified that he is no longer under consideration (p. 107).

i. The candidate must not be requested to give an answer by phone but be given ample time to prayerfully consider the call (p. 107).

14. The completion of the pulpit committee's responsibilities includes a number of important considerations.

a. A well-written formal letter of call should be promptly mailed to the candidate listing in detail all the agreements. A request for the minister to respond within a week or ten days should be included (p. 107; Appendix H).

b. The pulpit committee should be joined by the church in definite prayer for the man as he considers the call (p. 107).

c. A formal report of the minister's answer must be given to the church by way of announcement from the pulpit or at a business meeting. A written report is very much in order (p. 108).

d. Some group must be sure that all is in readiness for the arrival of the pastor and his family. The pulpit committee may have some responsibilities in this (p. 108).

e. Both formal and informal introductions of the pastor and his family to the church and community is part of the committee's responsibilities (pp. 108-9).

f. The terminal details of the committee will include the following items (p. 109):

(1) A written summary must be filed in the church archives.

(2) All confidential information on every man considered must be destroyed or returned to original sources.

(3) All expenses must be accounted for and all bills paid.

(4) A double check should be made to insure that every prospective pastor previously contacted has been notified that he is no longer being considered.

(5) Letters of thanks should be written to those who have given special help to the pulpit committee.

(6) Some type of communication should be sent to the church from which the new pastor came, assuring them of the committee's and their church's prayer concern as they now seek a new pastor.

The pulpit committee should be disbanded and pledge themselves to support the new pastor as he leads the church.

Appendix A

This appendix provides two self-study approaches. The first is to be used by the members of the church in an attempt to evaluate themselves, and from this determine the qualifications most needed in a pastor. The second is a detailed self-study designed to be used by assigned leaders of the church and/or denominational leaders.

A Look At Ourselves

1. Indicate areas of strength in our church's ministry. (Use 1 to indicate the strongest area, 2 to indicate the next strongest, etc. The higher the number, the lesser the strength.)
   _____ outreach (evangelism, visitation, etc.)
   _____ Christian education (Sunday school, etc.)
   _____ Christian education (youth and club work)
   _____ world missions
   _____ pulpit ministry
   _____ music ministry
   _____ community and social concerns

2. Enumerate the areas of greatest need in our church.
   _____ ministry to youth
   _____ spiritual growth
   _____ unity
   _____ concern for others
   _____ strong pulpit ministry

The letters, questionnaires, statements, and brochures given with the following appendixes are made up with fictitious names and situations, and are to be adjusted to meet the particular requirements of the inquiring church.

117

———— understanding of the Bible and the Christian way of life

———— informal fellowship, socials, outings, etc.

———— finances

3. As you see your church now, what areas of ministry do you feel should be emphasized, and for which a new pastor should be especially equipped? Enumerate them.

———— counseling

———— visitation

———— evangelism

———— teaching

———— pulpit ministry

———— administrative ability

———— community and social needs

———— ability to work with youth

4. To meet the needs of the church and its ministry, what do you feel should be your future pastor's emphasis in his preaching-teaching ministry?

———— topical studies

———— current cultural and societal concerns

———— world missions

———— evangelism

———— Bible exposition

———— studies for spiritual growth

NOTE: In all four questions, if two or more areas have equal importance, use the same number to give them equal rating.

Church Self-Study

I. PHILOSOPHY OF THE CHURCH

A. What is the Church?

B. Why does this local congregation exist?

C. What immediate and long-range goals have been determined from an understanding of this church's purpose?

D. What kind of pastor will best help this church meet its goals in the light of this mutually understood philosophy?

II. HISTORY OF THE CHURCH

A. Date and circumstances of the start of the church
   1. Date of actual organization
   2. Number of charter members
   3. Date of any reorganization
   4. Original name of the church and subsequent names
   5. Any change in denominational affiliation or status

B. Present building facilities
   1. How many building programs and expansions? Give details and dates.
   2. Year church entered present building

C. Equipment
   1. Date of installation of the following. Indicate whether new or used.
      a. organ
      b. hymn books
      c. pews
      d. pulpit furniture
      e. carpeting
      f. heating plant
      g. air conditioning equipment
      h. audiovisual equipment
      i. outdoor bulletin board
      j. other
   2. Any immediate plans for new equipment

D. Has the church merged with other churches in its lifetime? If so, with what churches?

E. Highest membership of the church. What year? Highest enrollment of the Sunday school. What year?

F. How many persons from the church have gone into full-time Christian service in the past ten years? Indicate whether members or not. Indicate what type of service.

G. Have there been any divisions or splinter groups leaving the church? If so, indicate what year(s).
   1. Do such divisions still trouble the church? In what way?
   2. Have such divisions affected the doctrinal position of the church?

H. Has the church sponsored any branch work? When? Give a brief description and indicate current membership and success of its ministry.

III. CHARACTER

A. Type of community served primarily (check categories which best describe)
    1. Rural village or small town
    2. Rural—open country
    3. Two-bedroom suburbia
    4. Three-four-five bedroom suburbia
    5. Specialty custom-built suburbia
    6. Urban-downtown community
    7. Inner city (transitional area of social, economic, racial change)

B. Location
    1. Residential community
       (primarily in an area of homes)
    2. Business area
    3. Industrial area
    4. Edge of community
    5. Small town
    6. Open country
    7. City—downtown
    8. Other

IV. EMPHASIS

What types of programs and service have been stressed over the past three years? Describe in paragraph form.

V. GOALS

What are the church's aims in the next two years in the area of:

A. Christian education
B. Membership growth
C. Conversions
D. Ministry to church's community
E. Missions
F. _____

VI. PROGRAM

Describe the church's current program. Give a paragraph description of each area and include the following: (1) purpose of the program or group; (2) major emphasis or program to reach purpose; (3) number of persons participating; (4) time and frequency of meetings or activities; (5) organizational relationship to the administration.

A. Sunday school
B. Youth fellowships, clubs
C. Children's meetings, clubs
D. Women groups
E. Men's brotherhood or fellowship
F. Community outreach
G. Discussion groups
H. Worship services
I. Other

VII. MEMBERSHIP

Prepare a church membership map. Use a good detail map with streets easily identified. Draw one- two- three- four- (possibly more) mile radius circles and indicate number of members living in each area. Use colored ink to indicate members' residences. (Do not use pins or tacks, as such a map cannot be mailed to the candidate.) Use red ink to indicate active members and blue to indicate inactive members.

A. Church membership: Indicate membership of the church over the past ten years.

YEAR	TOTAL	RESIDENT	NONRESIDENT

B. Sunday school enrollment and average attendance. Indicate for the past 10 years.
C. One other effective ministry such as youth clubs. Indicate name of ministry and number attending over the past 10 years.

VIII. FINANCES

A. How is the budget determined? Describe briefly.

B. How is the money obtained?
  1. Every member canvass
  2. Envelopes for every member
  3. Envelopes for those who desire them
  4. Offering plates passed at services. Indicate which services.
  5. Offering boxes at the entrance to the sanctuary
  6. Faith promises. For what part of the financial obligations of the church?
  7. Special seasonal offerings such as Easter, Christmas. How are these designated?
  8. Denominational cooperation. In what way?

C. Briefly describe any special features or successes in the financial thrust of the church.

D. Statistical summary of financial support. Indicate for the past ten years.

YEAR	CURRENT EXPENSES	BUILDING FUND	MISSIONS

IX. FACILITIES

A. Sanctuary. How many seats? _____

B. Sunday school facilities. Describe briefly. Include number of classrooms, etc.

C. Other. Describe.

D. Evaluate the adequacy of facilities for the church's current program.
   1. Very adequate and room for increased attendance
   2. Adequate for the present
   3. Inadequate. What plans are pending for providing better facilities?

X. STAFF

Check current positions and indicate whether full time, part time, paid or volunteer.

Position	Presently Filled	Vacant	Full Time	Part Time	Paid	Volunteer
Pastor						
Director of Christian Education						
Youth Pastor						
Business Manager						
Minister of Visitation						
Office Secretaries						
Sexton						
Associate Pastor						
Minister of Music						
Organist						
Other						

Are any changes or additions pending in the paid staff of the church? In what areas? When?

XI. RESPONSIBILITIES

A. What is the status of the community population growth in the five-mile areas immediately around the present church building?

1. Graph the population trends for the last ten years.
   a. declining
   b. static
   c. slowly increasing
   d. rapidly increasing
2. What reasons are evident for the population change?
3. What indications are there that the population increase or decrease will continue, level off, reverse?
4. If population is rapidly increasing, what is the cause? How long will this rapid increase continue? How is this determined?

B. What minority groups or ethnic groups is the church responsible for within the five-mile area of the present church building?
   1. What percentage is Caucasian? _____
   2. What percentage is black? _____
   3. What percentage is Spanish speaking? _____
   4. Other minority groups and percentages.
   5. What is the trend in population growth or decrease of the above ethnic or race groups within the five-mile area around the church building?
   6. What immediate and future ministries are planned to reach these people for Christ?

C. What topographical, industrial, housing, or other changes are anticipated in the area of the church?
   1. What industries plan to move in or out of the area?
   2. What housing projects are planned for the area?
   3. Is the housing deteriorating in the area?
   4. Are there any urban renewal projects planned or underway in the area?
   5. Are new expressways planned or under construction in the area?
   6. Interpret the above in regard to the church's ministries and plans.

D. What are the occupations of the persons in the church community?
   1. Percentage of professionals _____
   2. Percentage of white-collar workers _____

3. Percentage of blue-collar workers (skilled and semiskilled) _____

4. Percentage of laborers (unskilled) _____
5. Percentage of students _____
   a. undergraduate _____
   b. graduate _____
6. Percentage of unemployed and transient _____

E. What are the immediate and anticipated community needs? Describe briefly each category and any active or planned program to meet needs.

   1. Children
   2. Teen
   3. College and career
   4. Minority and/or racial groups

   5. Senior citizens
   6. Parents and home life
   7. Single adults
   8. Other

F. What other churches minister in the community within the five-mile area?

CHURCH NAME	DENOMINA-TION	AVERAGE ATTENDANCE A.M.	P.M.	MEMBER-SHIP

G. What agencies are available to assist the church or through which the church can serve to help meet community needs?

AGENCY NAME	TYPE OF SERVICE

H. Describe immediate, potential and/or possible programs in the following areas.
1. Overseas missions
2. Home missions
3. Branch church
4. Institutional and agency cooperation
5. Other

XII. MINISTERS

A. What pastors have served the church?

NAME	ADDRESS	NUMBER OF YEARS AS PASTOR	REASON FOR LEAVING

B. Provide same information for associate pastors, youth pastors, etc.

C. What provisions are made for the pastor of this church in the following categories?
1. Professional expenses
   a. book and periodical allowance
   b. automobile allowance
   c. conference and/or convention expenses
   d. continuing education allowance
   e. denominational service allowance
   f. other
2. Retirement and family protection
   a. hospitalization
   b. denominational retirement plan
   c. other

3. Basic compensation
   a. Housing allowance or parsonage value
   b. Utilities allowance
      (1) telephone
      (2) fuel
      (3) electric
      (4) gas
      (5) water and sewer
      (6) other
   c. Cash salary
4. Renewal opportunities
   a. vacation allotment
   b. special speaking engagements
   c. continuing education leave
   d. ministerial conference leave
5. Other provisions

XIII. EVALUATING THE STUDY

A. What does this study indicate to be the basic needs of the church?

B. What does this study indicate to be the strengths of the church?

C. What does this study indicate to be the weaknesses of the church?

D. What does this study indicate about the strengths and abilities needed in the next pastor?

E. What does this study say about the present program of the church?
   1. What needs to be terminated?
   2. What needs to be reevaluated?
   3. What needs to be upgraded?
   4. What needs to be added?

Appendix B

Here is a sample letter to request names of possible candidates, along with any information available concerning them. Each church will want to individualize its own letter and structure its own particular forms. The following is suggested as a guideline.

Dear Sir:

As of June 30, 1971, our congregation, the Community Church of Central City, Illinois, will be without a pastor.

The pulpit committee has been directed to you for names of possible candidates. We would greatly appreciate your assistance in suggesting available ministers you could recommend to us, along with a short background description and a statement of why you recommend each man to this particular church.

I am enclosing two brochures,* giving general information and statistical information of the varied ministries of our church. These may assist you in getting acquainted with us and thus help you in making recommendations.

Enclosed you will also find three copies of a recommendation form† which we would appreciate you using for providing us with information about suggested possible candidates.

We greatly appreciate any assistance you are able to provide.

Sincerely,

John Q. Smith
Secretary, Pulpit Committee
Community Church
Central City, Illinois

*See Appendix C.
†See Appendix D.

Appendix C

This appendix provides suggestions for brochures which could be xeroxed or mimeographed to enclose in the letter of Appendix B and the letter to prospective candidates of Appendix E. One is a general description of the church. The second is a summary of church and community information. The third is a suggestion for statistical information.

COMMUNITY CHURCH
Central City, Illinois

[Doctrinal statement]

THE MINISTRIES OF COMMUNITY CHURCH
Central City, Illinois

SUNDAY

9:45 A.M.

    Church in study
    Sunday school—21 classes
    Nursery—adult (3 adult classes)
    Five departments

11:00 A.M.

    Church in worship
    Morning worship
    Nursery
    Children's church (3- to 5-year-olds)
    Youth church (1st, 2d, 3d grades)

6:00 P.M.

    Church in training
    Nursery
    Sunbeams (4- and 5-yr. olds)
    Whirlybirds (1st, 2d, 3d grades)
    Jet Cadets (4th, 5th, 6th grades)
    Alpha Teens (jr. high)
    Omega Teens (sr. high)
    World Changers (Single adults, college and career)
    Parent's discussion group
    Senior citizens action group

7:00 P.M.

    Evening challenge and family hour

MONDAY

    6:30 P.M.

        Youth clubs
        Christian Service Brigade
        Pioneer Girls

WEDNESDAY

    7:15 P.M.

        Youth choir rehearsal and prayer meeting
        Church choir rehearsal and prayer meeting
        Bible study and prayer service

Vacation Bible school and summer camp programs are important facets of our summer ministries.

Our church gives to the following missions:

MISSION	MISSIONARY	COUNTRY

Offerings for general expenses and missions are received through the use of envelopes. Our annual missionary conference is held in March, when faith promises are made by our people to establish our missionary budget.

Third Wednesday each month—Women's missionary society

Fourth Thursday each month—Men's Brotherhood

Communion held first Sunday of each month

Church board, trustee board, deacon board meet first Tuesday of each month

Christian education committee meets bi-monthly

Sunday school staff meets bi-monthly, alternate months from C.E. committee above

The Community Church is located on the south side of Central City, five blocks west of Highway 12 at the intersection of Independence Road and Green Blvd. Its location is in a suburban residential area where most people own their own homes. We are about 40 miles north of the state capital.

Six other churches are located in Central City: First Presbyterian, Our Saviour Lutheran, Central Baptist, Church of God, United Methodist, and Seventh Day Adventist. Three other churches are located in the country near us but all over five miles away.

Our facilities include the original auditorium built in 1921, which was enlarged and completely remodeled seven years ago. The present auditorium seats 360 people and provides sufficient classrooms, office space, and a 60 ft. by 30 ft. multi-purpose room and kitchen. There is a full basement and the church is heated by a new hot water system. A sketch of the building is on the cover of this brochure.

Comunity Church is not denominationally affiliated but cooperates with many faith missions and joins each year with twelve other evangelical churches for an annual Crusade for Christ held during the summer months. We belong to the National Association of Evangelicals. Sunday school operates 12 months each year, and evening services are conducted every Sunday night, except during the Crusade. The men of the church conduct a service once a month at the Light and Hope Mission in downtown Central City.

COMMUNITY CHURCH
Central City, Illinois

The pulpit committee of Community Church has prepared the following summary of facts regarding the operation, organization, and current status of our church, plus pertinent information about our community.

COMMUNITY CHURCH

Organized as a local independent, evangelical congregation on March 1, 1952.

Present membership: 502

Average Sunday school attendance: 532

Average morning worship service attendance: 532

Average evening service attendance: 374

FACILITIES

Church building: 27,000 sq. ft.

Church property: 8.5 acres

Sanctuary seating capacity: 550

Building plans are in hand for expansion of sanctuary and additional Christian education facilities.

STAFF

Pastor, minister of youth, and C.E. Director

Church secretary (full time)

Custodian (full time)

Minister of music (part time)

CHURCH ADMINISTRATION

Advisory board (deacons, trustees and committee heads) for general administration of the church

Deacon board for spiritual oversight of the church

Trustee board for care of all physical aspects of the facilities

Sunday school superintendent, church clerk, treasurer, financial secretary

Missions council, Christian educational council

FINANCES

1974 income: $157,400, of which $47,000 was allocated to missions

CONGREGATION

The majority of our congregation are between 25 and 50 years of age. We have a large percentage of men in professional and semiprofessional occupations. Many have lived in our city for less than ten years, having moved to the community because of the rapid increase in industry.

COMMUNITY

Population: Rapid growth to over 165,000 from 52,000 in 1955.
Industry: Location of Expansion Industries Inc. and US Military Command, which employ over 51,000 persons. Greater diversification of industry insures continued community growth.

Statistical Information

Name of church _____
Name of pulpit committee secretary _____
Address _____ Phone _____
Population of church vicinity (three-mile radius) _____
Rate of growth in percent of church vicinity _____
Number of church members _____
Sunday school enrollment _____
Average attendance
   Sunday school _____
   A.M. worship _____
   P.M. worship _____
   Training hour _____
   Prayer meeting _____
   Youth choir _____
   Church choir _____
   Youth clubs _____
   Other _____
Rate of membership growth over past five years _____

Rate of attendance growth over past five years:

    A.M. service   _____

    P.M. service   _____

    Sunday school   _____

Seating capacity of sanctuary _____

Class capacity for Sunday school

    No. of classrooms _____

    Capacity of each classroom _____

Missionary budget over the past five years _____

Missionary giving over the past five years _____

Church budget over the past five years _____

Church giving over the past five years _____

Debt on church property _____

Debt on parsonage _____

Number of bedrooms in parsonage _____

Brief description of the administrative organization of the church

_____

_____

The church is (is not) incorporated. _____

Other salaried workers in the church _____

_____

Volunteer staff members of church _____

_____

Appendix D

A. GENERAL FORM

Below is a suggested recommendation form or ministerial appraisal form to be used by persons making recommendations to the pulpit committee concerning possible candidates. This can be sent along with the letter requesting names and also to references. If to references, the name and address of the candidate should be typed in the appropriate place on the form's first lines.

Pastoral Candidate Recommendation Form

(Please answer fully as many questions as your acquaintance with the man enables you.)

Name of potential candidate _____

Address _____ Phone _____

How long have you known this person? In what capacity? How recently have you been in contact with him?

What indicates to you that he is a deeply committed Christian?

Is he a soul winner?

What is his greatest interest or major emphasis?

Preaching	Music
Bible teaching	Visitation
Christian education	Counseling
Youth work	Other (specify)

In which areas of church work is he most proficient?

135

What capabilities does he have as a public speaker (preacher)?

With what age group does he work best?

What community interests and concerns have his past ministries indicated? Explain.

Is he flexible? Can he adapt to changing situations? Why do you say so? Can you illustrate by an example?

How does he react to problem situations?

Is he sensitive to the feelings of others? Why do you feel this way?

How well does he keep personal confidences?

Is there any personal trait, habit, or attitude which might hinder his ministry? Explain.

Is there any illness or ailment which might hinder him?

How does he handle his finances? Does he know how to live within his income?

Does his family, especially his wife, appear to be supportive of his ministry?

Comment on his family in regard to a Christian home.

How cooperative is he with the (denomination)?

Has your observation indicated his thinking concerning cooperative church endeavors and the ecumenical movement?

Do you know whether he is considering leaving his present ministry? If so, why?

What is his greatest asset?

What is his greatest weakness?

How would you rate his overall effectiveness as a pastor?

    Superior   Average

    Above average   Below average

In light of the information we have sent you about our church, do you recommend him as a possible pastor? Specifically why?

Please supply any additional information or comments.

Signature _____ Occupation _____

Position or office in your church _____Date _____

Please return this completed form to us by _____.
                                                   (Date)

Enclosed is an addressed and stamped envelope for your convenience. Thank you.

B. DENOMINATIONAL LEADER'S APPRAISAL FORM

The appraisal form for use by denomination leaders and district superintendents could vary somewhat from the general form above. Following is a suggestion. To help file forms, this one from denominational leaders should be on different colored paper than the general form.

Pastoral Candidate Appraisal Form

Please answer fully as many questions as your acquaintance with the man enables you.

Name of potential candidate _____

Address _____Phone _____

1. How long have you known him, and in what capacity?
2. How well does he cooperate with the denomination?
3. In what aspect of the pastorate is he most effective?
4. Has he shown ability, initiative, and creativity in program building in his pastorates? Please explain and give examples.
5. How does he rate as an administrator?
6. Does he have any idiosyncrasies or habits that are hindrances?
7. Are there any circumstances where he serves most efficiently? Any where he does not serve effectively?
8. How would you rate his overall pastoral work?

        Superior   Average

        Above average   Below average

Signature _____ Date _____

Position _____

Please return this completed form to us by _____.
                                                      (Date)
Enclosed is an addressed and stamped envelope for your convenience. Thank you.

C. SCHOOL APPRAISAL FORM

The evaluative form to be used by a seminary professor or
administrator should contain some specific questions different than
other inquiries. Below is a suggested form. Use still another color
of paper for this form than used for the two previous forms.

Pastoral Candidate Evaluative Form

Please answer fully as many questions as your acquaintance with
the man enables you.

Name of possible candidate _____

Address _____ Phone _____

1. What years did he attend your school?
2. How was he enrolled?
   Regular full-time student   Provisionally
   Part-time student   Other (specify)
3. Was he married at the time of enrollment? Any children?
4. Did he marry while at your school? Number of his children
   born while at your school _____.
5. What undergraduate work did he have before entering your
   school?
   What degree?
   From what college?
   Year degree received?
6. What program of studies did he pursue at your school?
   Did he change his program at any time?
   Did he have an intern experience? Where? How successful?
   What degree (or degrees) did he receive from your school?
   Did he receive any honors? Scholarships?
7. What was his relationship with the student body and faculty?
   Well-accepted by the students? Explain.
   Well-accepted by the faculty? Explain.
   Did he hold any class office? Which ones?

Did he serve as a faculty assistant?

Did he show any adverse reaction to regulations and/or policies of your school? Was he disciplined in any way?

8. Was he recommended for further graduate work? If so, what school or schools did he attend? When?

9. Do you have any recommendations on file by the faculty and/or placement office concerning his first or any subsequent pastorates?

10. Can you supply any information concerning his work since he left your school?

11. Can you offer other pertinent comments?

Signature _____ Date _____

Position _____

Please return this completed form to us by _____.

(Date)

Enclosed is an addressed and stamped envelope for your convenience. Thank you.

Appendix E

This appendix provides possible ways to make an initial inquiry with a prospective candidate. A self-evaluation application form (see Appendix F) may accompany the first letter for the prospect to return to the inquiring church if he is interested in pursuing the contact. This letter refers to two enclosures: a description of the church (see Appendix C) and an overview of the pastor. (See pp. 141-2.) The second letter of this appendix introduces a less involved preliminary questionnaire which could be followed by the more in-depth application of Appendix F if the preliminary response so indicates.

LETTER OF INQUIRY

Form 1

Dear Mr. Minister:

The Reverend Arthur Ample has completed an eight-year pastorate here at the Community Church of Central City and has resigned to become associate pastor of the Open Door Church, Middle City, Ohio. A pulpit committee has been selected by the church to seek and recommend a successor to Mr. Ample. On behalf of the pulpit committee, I am writing you.

The Community Church of Central City has a membership of 356 with a general expense budget of $47,000 and a mission budget of $22,000. The Sunday school has an enrollment of 420 with an average attendance of 390. Our pastor receives a cash salary of $12,000, the allotted amount for the denominational retirement plan, an automobile allowance of $1,000 and a $500 provision for utilities. A three-bedroom parsonage, built in 1956, is provided. Our church cooperates fully with the _____ denomination and we are interested in securing a pastor who can participate happily in this denominational relationship.

Your name has been suggested to us as one who would give us good leadership and who possessed qualities to help meet the needs of our church. Without any commitment, either on your part or that of our church, we would like to know whether you would consider further communication concerning pastoral leadership here at our church. Enclosed is a brochure giving basic information concerning our church* and a statement of how we view the pastoral position in our church. If, after reading these, you feel led of God to investigate further, please fill out the enclosed evaluative application form and return it to us at your earliest convenience. If you desire further information, please feel free to contact us.

Sincerely,

Fred Faithful, chairman
Pulpit Committee
Community Church

A Pastor of God's Own Choosing
For Community Church

Ephesians 4:11

We feel that our pastor should be a shepherd for our people. We want him to be an example for us in godliness and Christian living, and thus lead us closer to the Saviour. We feel that the pulpit ministry is a very important part of his work. Thus we would expect our pastor to spend four or five mornings in his study. We want sermons which are saturated with Scripture and have relevant application for daily living. We feel that our pastor should teach and train our people in Bible study, doctrinal understanding, and effective evangelism. He should have a genuine interest and concern for the youth of our church as well as the senior citizens. Our pastor, along with the deacons, should have a real burden for a visitation ministry, in homes, institutions and hospitals, including an evangelistic outreach. It would be wise for our pastor to establish counseling hours when individuals can make appointments to meet him in his study. We feel that our

*See Appendix C.

pastor should encourage the people of the church to be involved in the work of the church. He should be willing and able to train people for assigned tasks. We feel our pastor should be interested in a membership of spiritual quality rather than just quantity. We want a membership of born-again people who are growing in Christ.

LETTER OF INQUIRY

Form 2

Rev. Possible Candidate
20 Plain St.
Central City, Illinois

Dear Possible Candidate:

Since Pastor Lawrence Olson resigned, it has been the prayerful concern of the church that God might lead us to His man to be our pastor. Your name has been recommended as a possible candidate.

If your heart responds to this letter, we invite you to write a short statement to the enclosed questionnaire. This is not an examination, but rather a practical method of becoming acquainted. You may have questions to ask of us. Feel free to raise them. Your response will be held in confidence.

We will wait to hear from you.

Cordially yours in Christ,

John Jones
Secretary, pulpit committee
enc.

Questionnaire for Prospective Candidates

The prayerful concern of the Community Church at this time is to find God's man as our pastor. Having stood for a conservative position, we feel it is important to discover a man who can wholeheartedly enter into this tradition. Thus a mutual need exists. You will want to ask questions, and we are desirous to know your mind and heart. Therefore, we invite you to write a short statement on the following questions.

1. *Statement of Faith*
   Do you accept the enclosed statement of faith without reser-

vation? Where do you place yourself in respect to the Calvinist and Arminian traditions? Enlarge on your view of the Bible, the Holy Spirit, the charismatic movement, and the second coming of Christ.

2. *Loyalty*
Would you be loyal to our association/conference in the measure that they are true to Christ?

3. *Priorities*
List your work schedule priorities 1,2,3 on the following: personal preparation, preaching, administration, visitation. What part would you take in the area of Christian education?

4. *Social Issues*
What is your approach to social issues such as war, peace, race, politics?

5. *Christian Behavior*
How would you handle problems that involve Christian behavior in the area of questionable things?

6. *Interdenominational Cooperation*
What is your attitude toward interdenominational cooperation such as local church councils, National Association of Evangelicals, Billy Graham Crusades?

7. *Training and Service*
Tell us of your academic training and the names of the churches you have served.

8. *Family*
What is your concept of the family in its relation to the church? Can over-involvement endanger family life?

9. *Staff*
How would you handle your church staff?

10. *The Church*
What is the purpose of the local church?

Appendix F

An application form for prospective candidates is something that is not common today. Its value has not been tested, but there is indication that such a form can save much time in the initial steps of the candidating procedure. This form could be changed slightly and used for any paid staff position in the church.

Information Request Form

PERSONAL

Name _____ Social Security No. _____
(print)   First   Middle   Last
                              Birth date _____

Present address _____
                Street   City   State   Zip
Phone No. _____ Height _____ Weight _____

Are you:

Single?   Separated? Date_____
Engaged?   Divorced? Date_____
Married? Date_____   Widowed? Date_____

Number of children _____ Ages _____

US citizen? _____ Dependents other than wife and children

_____

Spouse's occupation _____

Spouse's employer and address _____

Names of friends or relatives who are members of this church ___

_____

144

POSITION

Today's date _____ Position interested in _____

Date of availability _____

Carefully but briefly define your philosophy of the local church.

What is your understanding of the purpose of the local church?

Summarize the goals you have set for the next five years in your present pastorate.

Indicate general goals you would set for Community Church if you were its pastor, based on the information of the self-study enclosed.

EDUCATION

	NAME AND LOCATION	CIRCLE LAST YEAR COMPLETED	DEGREE AND DATE RECEIVED	MAJOR SUBJECT	RANK IN CLASS*
Elementary		5 6 7 8			U M L
High School		1 2 3 4			U M L
College		1 2 3 4			U M L
College		1 2 3 4			U M L
Graduate School		1 2 3 4			U M L
Other		1 2 3 4			U M L

*U—Upper 25%   M—Middle 50%   L—Lower 25%

Now attending _____undergraduate school _____graduate school.

Degree objective _____

List college activities and offices held

What was your undergraduate major?

Please list any and all community, social, church, political, and professional organizations that you belong to. List offices held.

EMPLOYMENT HISTORY

List previous major secular employers (last employer first).

Name of company   Dates employed (mo. & yr.)

Address   From _____ To _____

Description of work and type   Starting salary _____
   of business: Final salary _____

Your position(s)   Supervisor's name and title

Reason for leaving

(Use form above for other employment)

List all previous church or church-related employment.

Name of church _____ Dates employed (Mo. & yr.)

Address _____ From _____ To _____

Position _____ Starting salary _____

If not senior pastor, give the name
   of supervisor and title

_____ Final salary _____

Reason for leaving

(Use form above for all other church-related employment)

DOCTRINE

On a separate sheet of paper please briefly explain, with biblical undergirdings, your views, beliefs, and convictions concerning the following doctrines and subjects:

The Trinity
The Holy Spirit
Inspiration and authenticity
   of Scripture
Soteriology
Eschatology
Dispensationalism
Ecumenical movement
Cooperative evangelism
Denominationalism
Tithing
Church discipline
Communion (Lord's Supper)
Morality and ethics
The Christian life
   (separation)

Sanctification
Gift of tongues & healing
Gifts of The Holy Spirit
Evangelism and its place in
   the Church
Missions
Social work as it relates to
   the church
Divorce and remarriage for
   the Christian
Jesus Christ (His deity and
   humanity)
Virgin birth of Christ
Baptism

Please enclose a copy of your ordination biographical sketch, call to the ministry, and doctrinal statement. Indicate any changes in your beliefs or views since that time.

ORDINATION

What year were you ordained? _____ What church requested your ordination? _____ Any changes in your ordination status? _____ If yes, explain.

Have you ever been censured by a denomination or church? _____. If yes, when? _____ Explain.

Have your ordination credentials ever been withdrawn or revoked? _____ If yes, when? _____ Explain.

What group (denomination, fellowship or church) now holds your ordination credentials? Address of this group _____

PREACHING CURRICULUM

In what area(s) does your preaching strength lie? Briefly outline your preaching curriculum for the past six months.

SKILLS

List and explain any additional skills you have, such as craftsman or musician.

MILITARY

Present draft status _____ If exempt, why? _____
Veteran of US Armed Forces? _____ What branch? _____
Date inducted _____ Last rank attained _____ Date discharged _____ Type of discharge _____ Member of National Guard? _____ Reserves? _____

PHYSICAL RECORD

List any physical limitations or chronic illness _____

Were you ever injured? _____ Give details _____

Have you been hospitalized? _____ When? _____ For
how long? _____ For what reason? _____

_____

Have you ever had psychiatric treatment or counseling? Explain.

Have you any defect in hearing? _____ In vision? _____
In speech? _____

Has any application for life insurance, hospitalization, or retirement insurance been rejected due to physical reasons? _____
If yes, explain.

REFERENCES

Give the names of three persons not related to you, and not listed
in any other part of this form, whom you have known at least two
years.

NAME	ADDRESS	BUSINESS	YEARS ACQUAINTED
1.			
2.			
3.			

SPECIAL INFORMATION

Do you have any sideline business or income-producing work?
_____ If so, explain.

List books you have written or are now writing _____

_____

List the books you have read in the past 12 months _____

_____

Have any prior employers received wage assignments, demands,
or garnishments concerning you? _____

Please list the hours of services of the church you now serve

    Sunday school _____

    Morning worship _____

    Evening worship _____

Please mention any dates when you will *not* be in your pulpit

_____

I understand that my past employment and education records will be investigated by the church, and I hereby grant permission for this to be done, along with verification of any other information noted herein. I also agree to submit to a medical examination, if requested.

Signature _____ Date _____

Appendix G

Here is the pastoral job specification written by Robert Rox-burgh, pastor of the Glenbard Baptist Church of Glen Ellyn, Illinois. He says the following concerning this job description:

> One of the greatest things that happened to me in my ministry was not even quite a spiritual thing. The chairman of the board at my church, even before I was called, asked me to do one thing which actually came out of the business world, but was relevant and important. He said, "Pastor, I want you to write out a job description as you see the ministry and I want to take it back to the board. I then want to tell the people that these are the terms under which you will come to our church." I began to outline the things to which I felt God had called me uniquely, as a pastor of the Gospel of Jesus Christ. I defined areas in which I would not work, areas that I had long felt were not in my particular area of ministry. And, very honestly, I have not, except for the rare occasion, stepped beyond the outlines of this job description. I have worked in the freedom of this frame of reference and I have not been criticized for failing to do certain things which were not expected of me from the beginning.

The Ministry of the Pastor

1. PREACHING AND TEACHING—1 Timothy 4:11-16; 1 Timothy 5:17-18

The most important aspect of the ministry as I see it is to *teach* and *preach* the Word of God. This is the New Testament way to build the saints. John 17:17 is the theme I think God blesses.

The material in this appendix is quoted from "The Layman and His Church" by Robert Roxburgh, *United Evangelical Action* 26, no. 11 (January 1968):8-10, official publication of the National Association of Evangelicals. Used by permission.

Practical: This concept would take a large part of the work week. The study would be the workshop.

2. THE SHEPHERD—"feed (i.e., pastor) my sheep"

The ministry is to those who are sick and those who are well.

A. The sick
  i. *In body.* Visit those who are in hospital or laid aside at home.
  ii. *In mind.* Counsel, within the limits of my ability, any with problems of a psychological or sociological nature. Refer counselees to more adequate and professional help, etc. There are many alcoholics and psychotics that the church does not try to reach. There can be a ministry here for the eventual salvation of souls.
  iii. *In soul.* Counsel on the pastoral level with those who have a spiritual problem, such as temptations, doubts, etc.

Practical: This runs a close second in time consumption and is vital in giving content to the preaching and teaching ministry. The Word must come alive with answers to those who during the week are beset with problems and have come to church on Sunday to hear the Lord's answers given through His servant. The congregation must see that the Pastor's call to a church involves his person-to-person involvement with people in the community.

B. The well
  The pastor, of course, ministers to a majority of normal people who gather to worship the Lord. An important task is to prepare the worship services in such a way that the congregation is deeply impressed with the presence of God, etc.

Practical: Hymns, prayers, etc. should be prepared. Consultation with such folk as the choir leader, song leader, organist all help to make the services meaningful. To have an excellent sermon and a poorly planned service is bad.

C. Prayer
  In the role of shepherd, the pastor must bring before the throne of grace the many needs, problems, and concerns of the congregation.

Practical: Beyond his own personal quiet time, part of the pastoral responsibility is to use the time in his study for intercession for his people. Our generation has lost the concept of saintliness. The pastor must show the way.

3. THE EVANGELIST—2 Timothy 4:5

He must have a personal concern for the lost souls of men.

Practical: The leading of men to Christ will come about through visiting new families that attend church service, counseling non-church people who seek help and through the Sunday ministry. But primarily and most effectively, the pastor's responsibility will be to train laymen to become evangelists (see sec. 4).

4. THE OVERSEER—Acts 15:23; 1 Peter 5:1-4

While there is, of course, a sense in which all church work is spiritual, we will make here the understood difference between administrative and spiritual leadership. The pastor's concern is for the general spiritual tone of the church. He wants to develop the quality of teaching and improve methods of soul growth.

Practical: He works very closely with the deacons in maintaining scriptural standards and doctrines. The deacons are his right arm in the task of upholding biblical ethics, love, and morality in the church membership.

Practical: From years of training and experience the pastor will be vitally concerned for the areas of Christian education, missions, etc. He will come to the major committee meetings fully prepared to suggest, listen, and challenge. There his personal work in the committee will end. The implementation of ideas, recruiting of workers, establishments of programs, etc., must be done by the lay people. This is the congregation's church. It is the people who must carry much of the work in these areas.

Perhaps a better word than *overseer* is *coach*. The pastor is not *the* team, but the coach of the team who trains and equips as many as he can to do the work of the ministry.

A church is successful to the degree that the pastor is successful in involving the laymen in the total effort of the church. It has been my common practice to take laymen with me when I visit, so their in-service training for evangelism, counsel, etc., is effected.

Part of the great tragedy of the ministry is that the pastor is forced to do work which eliminates his time for the very work to which God and the church called him. This is not a matter of the pastor being too proud to clean the church windows, but a matter of priorities in the light of eternal verities.

N.B. The following areas I would *not* consider my responsibility. (Of course, I would always maintain a prayerful interest.)

1. Finances (i.e., books. I will preach on tithing, of course)
2. Building maintenance
3. Printing and office work, bulletin, etc.
4. Use of facilities (i.e., permission to use, say, the kitchen for a party.
5. Purchasing of supplies (e.g., new hymn books). Salesmen should know not to come to the pastor, but go rather to the elected laymen (trustee?).
6. Conducting, moderating business meetings, or chairing *any* committee.

As a pastor, I have always worked closely with the elected leaders of the church (i.e., the elders and deacons), leading them to see that I am an elder among elders, a leader among equals who, themselves, must bear the responsibility of the church for evangelism, missions, spiritual life, discipline, outreach, growth. This has been best accomplished by a definite executive approach; that is, by going to lunch with a committee chairman and brainstorming with him *before* his committee meeting, by taking the leaders on weekend retreats for prayer, challenge, orientation, goal-setting and implementation. I have deemed it wise to "sell" the deacons (elders, etc.) on an idea and allow them to sell the congregation. I have, by this method, been able to keep away from direct administrative leadership conflict with the church, or in any program.

A helpful way to clearly outline a job description is to outline a "pastor's schedule." I have made notes for clarity as to a typical work week I have found common over the years.

TYPICAL WORK WEEK

Monday-Friday

8:00 A.M.—12:00 noon in office

The work at the office would be as follows (not in any particular order).

1. Prayer
2. Bible study and sermon preparation
3. Read poetry, literature, history, current events, religious trends, write articles, etc.
4. Formulate ideas for the church program. Have suggestions for committees.

For me, personally, I find that fifteen hours on sermons and five hours on a Bible study is minimum. This comes to over 20 hours each week.

During the office hours there should be no phone calls before noon, except emergencies. All calls can be made to the parsonage or the church secretary, if such exist. Urgent messages can be relayed from these sources.

12:00 P.M.—2:00 P.M., lunch

2:00—4:00 P.M., visitation (Tues., Wed., Thurs. only)

Hospitals, sick families where the husband works nights, etc.

6:00—10:00 P.M. (approx.)—*Tuesday, Wednesday, Thursday Evenings*

Tuesday and Thursday—office hours for counseling at the church.

Those with problems can call any time of day or night, and I will come. However, to keep counseling meaningful and effective, these hours will be kept for consultation in my office.

When there is no counseling on these evenings, I will be out visiting.

Wednesday evening is prayer service, committees, etc.

N.B. Monday, Friday, Saturday evenings will be spent with my family, and I am very anxious to maintain this responsibility to them.

Saturday, my day off

Sunday, duties obvious

Such a schedule is flexible but only when demands to adjust are meaningful.

Total expected work hours per week—55

I believe the pastor who spends all his time at church, to the neglect of self and family, is not only busy, but barren.

Committee Meetings. If all meetings were held on Wednesdays (deacons 1st of month, etc.), then I could be at a meeting each week and still do my work adequately. The pastor would be at each scheduled meeting of the major committees.

Appendix H

The letter of call, sometimes referred to as the letter to the pastor-elect, should be concise and should include all pertinent information. It is a type of contract. Something like the following should be used.

The Reverend Paul T. Pastor
Upper Center, California

Dear Mr. Pastor:

With gratitude to God, I have the pleasure to inform you that by 231 positive and 7 negative votes, the members of the Community Church of Central City, Illinois, on March 20, 1974, extended you a call to become their pastor. The spirit of the church members in accepting the pulpit committee's recommendation was one of enthusiasm as they thanked God for the consensus directed by the Holy Spirit. We hope your response to this letter will be the same.

The terms of the call, as mutually agreed upon during the pulpit committee's conference with you on March 1, are as follows.

The church will provide:

1. Annual cash salary of $12,000
2. Parsonage use, estimated annual rental value $3400
3. Utilities' allowance of $500 per year
4. Annual automobile expense allowance of $1000
5. Full premium payment to the denomination's pastoral retirement program
6. Full family coverage for hospitalization and surgery
7. Coverage of moving expenses from your present residence to the parsonage in Central City

8. Expenses as a delegate to the denominational annual conference, district conference, and ministerial association conference.
9. One-month paid vacation, the time of which to be determined by you.
10. Opportunity for at least one week's study leave each year, cumulatively if desired, and $100 per year for such educational expenses.

We understand that as our pastor-elect you agree:

1. To accept the pastoral leadership of the Community Church, Central City, Illinois, and all the responsibilities related thereto, as stated in the enclosed pastoral job specification, beginning May 1, 1974.
2. To the by-laws of the Community Church, Central City, Illinois, which states that the pastoral relationship may be terminated by either pastor or church upon a one-month notice.

We have endeavored to carefully outline the arrangements implicitly in this call. If, however, you desire further information, please phone us collect. We join you in prayer as you consider this call and wait your written reply within the next two weeks.

By order of the church,

Ernest Effort
Church Clerk

Notes

CHAPTER 1

1. J. B. Lightfoot, *Saint Paul's Epistle to the Philippians.* (London: Macmillan, 1885), pp. 92, 192, 207.

CHAPTER 2

1. T. Harwood Pattison, *For the Work of the Ministry* (Philadelphia: Amer. Bapt. Pub. Soc., 1907), p. 65.
2. Edward T. Hiscox, *The Hiscox Standard Baptist Manual* (Valley Forge: Judson, 1965, 1967), p. 56.
3. Henry Wilder Foote, *The Minister and His Parish* (New York: Macmillan, 1923), p. 9.
4. Albert W. Palmer, *The Minister's Job* (Chicago: Willett, Clark, 1937), p. 92.
5. *Moody Monthly Magazine* 69(November 1968):10.
6. Lloyd H. Goetz, "Filling the Vacancy," in *Calls and Vacancies,* ed. Oscar H. Reinboth (St. Louis: Concordia, 1956), p. 42.
7. Washington Gladden, *The Christian Pastor and the Working Church* (New York: Scribner, 1911), p. 75.
8. Ibid., p. 76.
9. William R. McNutt, *Polity and Practice in Baptist Churches* (Philadelphia: Judson, 1935), p. 85.
10. Gaines S. Dobbins, *Building Better Churches: A Guide to the Pastoral Ministry* (Nashville: Broadman, 1947), p. 322.
11. Ibid., p. 23.
12. Washington Gladden, ed., *Parish Problems* (New York: Century, 1887), pp. 22-23.
13. Ibid., p. 23.
14. Horace Worth, *The Art of Candidating* (Boston: Printed for private circulation, 1907), pp. 58-60.
15. Ibid., p. 59.
16. *Christian Life* 31, no. 7(November 1961):12.

CHAPTER 3

1. Walter E. Schuette, *The Minister's Personal Guide* (New York: Harper, 1953), p. 16.
2. Henry Wilder Foote, *The Minister and His Parish,* p. 15.
3. Washington Gladden, *The Christian Pastor and the Working Church* (New York: Scribner, 1911), p. 76.
4. Ibid., pp. 76-77.
5. Foote, p. 12.

6. Lloyd H. Goetz, "Filling the Vacancy," in *Calls and Vacancies,* ed. Oscar H. Reinboth (St. Louis: Concordia, 1967), p. 48.
7. Ambrose Bailey, *The Pastor in Action* (New York: Round Table, 1939), p. 15.
8. Francis Wayland and H. L. Wayland, *Life of Francis Wayland,* p. 118, as quoted by T. Harwood Pattison, *For the Work of the Ministry,* p. 77.
9. Foote, p. 17.
10. Gaines S. Dobbins, *Building Better Churches,* p. 317.
11. Pattison, p. 79.
12. Gaines S. Dobbins, *The Church Book* (Nashville: Broadman, 1951), p. 56.

CHAPTER 4

1. Class notes in Persuasion in Preaching, by Lloyd M. Perry, Trinity Evangelical Divinity School.
2. Gaines S. Dobbins, *Building Better Churches,* p. 313.
3. Leonard E. Hill, "What the Pulpit Committee Should Know," *Church Administration* 6 (June 1964):10.
4. Leonard E. Hill, *Your Work on the Pulpit Committee* (Nashville: Broadman, 1970), p. 44.
5. Lloyd M. Perry and Edward J. Lias, *A Manual of Pastoral Problems and Procedures* (Grand Rapids: Baker, 1964), p. 15.
6. Henry Wilder Foote, *The Minister and His Parish,* p. 9.

CHAPTER 5

1. Leonard E. Hill, "What a Pulpit Committee Should Know About His Church," *Church Administration* 6 (April 1964), 28.
2. Henry Wilder Foote, *The Minister and His Parish,* p. 13.
3. Robert Roxburgh, "The Layman and His Church, Part I," *United Evangelical Action* 26, no. 11 (January 1968):8-10; "The Layman and His Church, Part II," *United Evangelical Action* 26 (February 1969):11-12.
4. Leonard E. Hill, "Where to Get Help—In Search of Prospective Pastors," *Church Administration* 6 (May 1964):25.
5. Ibid.
6. Foote, p. 10.
7. Ambrose Moody Bailey, *The Pastor in Action,* p. 15.
8. The Commission on the Ministry, American Baptist Convention, *Calling a Baptist Minister,* rev. ed (Valley Forge: November 1967), p. 12.
9. Charles R. Erdman, *The Work of the Pastor* (Philadelphia: Westminster, 1924), p. 14. For consideration of what the candidating pastor should ask the church, see Gerald W. Gillaspie, *The Restless Pastor* (Chicago: Moody, 1974).
10. Leonard E. Hill, "How to Test Recommendations," *Church Administration* 6 (August 1964): 19.
11. Ibid.
12. Adapted from Leonard Hill, *Your Work on the Pulpit Committee,* p. 15.
13. Foote, p. 11.
14. Hill, p. 21.

CHAPTER 6

1. Leonard E. Hill, "When You Vote to Call a Pastor," *Church Administration* 6(October 1964):31.